CHECK THE RHYME

an anthology of female poets & emcees

Edited by
DuEwa Frazier

CHECK THE RHYME

an anthology of female poets & emcees

Lit Noire Publishing

New York

Published by
Lit Noire Publishing
P.O. Box 26183
Brooklyn, NY 11201
www.duewaworld.com

Copyright © 2006, 2012, 2013 DuEwa Frazier, DuEwa M. Frazier
Contributors retain the copyright © for each of their works.

3rd Edition, Revised

Layout: DuEwa Frazier
Front Cover Design: Jonathan Gullery

Library of Congress Control Number: 2006905402

Check the rhyme: an anthology of female poets and emcees / edited by DuEwa Frazier.
Includes biographical references.

ISBN-10: 0-971-90525-8
ISBN-13: 978-0-9719052-5-2
    I.   Frazier, DuEwa

Printed in the United States of America

10 9 8 7 6 5 4 3 2 1

Dedicated to all the little girls who grew up to become women who create a new world, through the power of voice, and the defiant stroke of the pen.

And for Ntozake Shange, June Jordan, lindamichellebaron and Sonia Sanchez – the first women poets I ever read.

Introduction

It was 2003 when I first thought of the concept for an anthology that would solely feature the poetry of women writers. In my travels and work as a poet, writer, teacher and performance artist I had come into contact with so many dynamic young poets, as well as women who consider themselves to be lyricists or emcees. I wanted to gather the work of these women writers, in order to tell a story that would serve as the antidote to the current hip hop videos, lyrics and personalities which I believed had been dominating and negatively affecting our artistic culture, our mindset and our relationships. I came up with the title *Check the Rhyme* after reflecting on the value of both poetry in print and poetry that is performed by poets and lyricists alike. I was also equally inspired by the hip hop group Tribe Called Quest, whose music was the soundtrack to my late teen years and early adult life.

Check the Rhyme is not a publication created to denounce hip hop in any way. Instead, this publication reveals a new vision for the hip hop generation, and others, as the poets give voice to our concerns for: our culture, our world, our communities and the emotional, spiritual and physical issues we as women, as people face, on a day to day basis.

What most concerns me now, as an artist and educator is how to help our female youth develop and maintain their consciousness, self respect, dignity and intellect. One of the ways I can best model this is through my art, and by supporting creative work that will inspire our youth. *Check the Rhyme* is a publication that was created to serve as a tool to inspire young girls to write. How are our female youth fairing in the face of such blatant messages and images in today's popular culture? I see young girls' struggles everyday in my work as a secondary school teacher: the female students who label themselves "bitches" and "hos," the female students who expose their bodies to boys seeking attention, the female students who believe they are "ugly" and do not matter.

Who told them it was okay to reduce themselves to being ugly, bitches and hos? Who is going to help turn it around for them, to affirm that they are whole, intelligent and beautiful as they are - whether or not they wear the latest name brand clothes, call themselves derogatory names or show their body parts to boys for attention?

The contributors in this book paint a picture of what it is like to be a woman today - a creative thinking woman, regardless of age, race, class or educational background.

Check the Rhyme features poetry, which reveals a diverse consciousness within the themes poets have presented. Hurricane Katrina is an occurrence that will forever change our lives and the way we help one another in the face of extreme circumstance. Hurricane Katrina revealed to us the way those in authority treat people who are deemed invaluable, because of race and/or class. Poets wrote about their perspective on this tragedy.

Poet, Tiffany Woods Bennett tells of a pledge to assist those persons affected most by Hurricane Katrina in "The Sun Shall Rise Again":

This is one time I will actually follow through
Together we will reconstruct, once again you will reign
I'm choosing in this wake to not let your dead be in vain

Other themes in *Check the Rhyme* include: perspectives on beauty and self esteem; empowerment for youth; desire for a transformed hip hop culture; reflections on loving and longing; the memory and meaning of home; perspectives on the state of our society; artistic and political contributions of legends of and before our time; abuse and healing from violence; lessons from and memories of family; love of jazz; Black history; and spirituality among other themes.

This book, which features some of the most diverse and intriguing female poets and emcees of our time, says that women have a voice that will not be silenced or denied! That we will create images and art that informs our communities and sets an example of excellence in the face of degradation and mediocrity on any level. We have those women writers and other artists who came before us, to serve as our role models and gate-keepers of a culture we seek to uplift and maintain.

Lit Noire Publishing is an independent publisher, with no investors or sponsors to date, making *Check the Rhyme* a milestone and groundbreaking publication. As a service to each community I am a part of – women, women of color, African Americans, writers, activists and educators - I am proud to publish and promote women writers who are striving each day to maintain their art and serve the world through their creative gifts.

Get lost within these pages and dream a new world for yourself!

DuEwa Frazier
Editor & Publisher
September 2012

Acknowledgements

I wish to thank my family for their continued support. I wish to thank all of the poets who contributed their work on these pages, for this project would have been impossible without them. I must thank writer's listserves and websites for assisting me in spreading the call for submission to *Check the Rhyme*: Kalamu Ya Salaam (e-drum), Pittsburgh's The Soul Pitt African American writer's website, Okera Ras (Kwanzaa Media), B-Gyrl.com, Reginald Harris (Cave Canem listserve), Spiral Bridge Poets, Backlist, Mosaic Books and many other listserves.

Also thank you to Nubian Heritage Bookstores, Howard University Bookstore, Queens Book Fair, QBR Harlem Book Fair, House of Brown, Sisters Uptown Bookstore, Bowery Poetry Club, The Nuyorican Poet's Cafe, the Challenge Group and Courier Life Newspapers, Morningside Alliance for support of my books and events. Special thanks to Tachelle Wilkes, Michelle Sewell and the editors of Feminist Review.

TABLE OF CONTENTS

Chapter 7 - Haiku

Chapter 8 - Identity and the Mirror of Self

Chapter 9 - I Dream of Hip Hop

Chapter 10 - Jazz Journey

Chapter 11- Longing & Memories of Love

Chapter 12 - Performing Poetry & Praising Poets

Chapter 1
About Hair

PLAITS
You never wanted me to wear the night
with empty hands
So I filled them with the peeling layer of your back
I know every dead and living inch of your body
Which part of your tongue was used to taste sourness
And which part was sharp enough to saw
I've cut my hair to cut you out because
You were never brave enough to take a scalpel
To the cancerous parts
I've cut my knees enough from the begging
Sacrificed enough words
While you grow your hair long enough for braiding

ROOTED

beautiful black man
darker than the rich soil you till
bluer than the sweet pain in your heart
you come to me, bone tired and sleepy
w/a comb in one hand, a fragrant jar in the other
i motion for you to sit on the floor
then crush you between my ample thighs
dividing your jungle of tangled roots
i gently oil your scalp
taking from the blue dollop of afro sheen
thick and unmoving on the back of my hand
part/scratch/grease
part/scratch/grease
part/scratch/grease
you are fast asleep when i
etch fertile rows in your hair
situate front strands in slick fingers
and braid tight enough for you to wake
w/a frown flitting across your divine black face
an iridescent line of drool escaping the corner of your
mouth.

HER HAIRSTORY
Straight from infancy
they all stared at me
trying to sneak and see
what the texture of my "Hair" might be.
Friends and family would ooh! and wow!
at my drooling smile
or scream surprise at the gleam in my eyes,
but in the end they couldn't pretend
or hide, how much they truly cared
about the goodness or the badness
of my hair.
So It was of course decided from there
whether I would
lift them up or let them down,
whether they could sing or frown
about what was growing
on top of my baby crown
Was it slick and straight
crimp and curly
or simply bald,
because even bald was better then nappy
no way I'd ever be happy,
if my kinky edges continued to grow
happiness, I'd never know.
Never bothered to see
that the bubbling brown beauty of me
was the true texture of my identity.
And my momma, she knowing no better
brought into the myth

that life for me would truly be bad
it made her sad
that my hair wasn't good.
So she proceeded to saturate my scalp
with baby oils and vaselines
until I portrayed the visions in her dreams
of a chocolate child with long flowing locs
that didn't bead up
and didn't knot.
She'd brush and comb and braid and plait
until my ponytails swung down my back.
and I was barley beyond the toddlers age
before she progressed and moved on
to the pressing comb stage
with her gripping me tightly
between her knees and burning flat
what she called my "peas."
my "kitchen" or "backyard"
as I often heard her say
had to stay straight for the rest of the day.
From then on and all through my adolescent years
I'd sit and cry my silent tears,
and try to overcome my fears,
of never being seen as me,
And even now
being the adult that I am

people still don't understand
that who I am is not my hair
a person of color
and pride
and worth
who God put here to decorate this earth.
it doesn't equate all that I have to share
about the beautiful, brown, blackness of me
it's only a part of the package you see
My cultural creation
of skin, style, language and hair
are all parts of myself to be cherished and shared.
So whether I'm wearing a wig
weaved, braided or completely relaxed
I will no longer allow myself to be socially attacked
by those who don't know me
and those who can't see
that all of my blackness
represents me

Chapter 2
Black History

THE SOUL OF A WOMAN

Gaze into the deepest essence of me
and you shall find the soul of
African-American history
In me, you will discover the leadership of Harriett
Tubman, for it is my greatest desire to lead the lost souls
of the Lord into the Promised Land
and when faced with adversity, I shall rise again and
again to obey the Lord's commands
my will to thrive and survive shall spread like fire, as
others conspire to join me.

As my femininity is boasted across the stage
demanding your respect and praise, you will find the
aura of Dorothy Dandridge.
For I shall dance and sing my way into even the most
callous hearts
maneuvering my way to the top of the charts
using my God given gifts as master of the arts
opening door after door, because with me is where
acceptance starts.

Observe my determination and abilities
and you will find the presence of none other than
Phillis Wheatley
For I have a voice that will be heard
and a spiritual gift of having a way with words
I will write and recite every chance I get, so that
generations to come should never forget.

My love of jazz and my bodacious pizzazz
will have you look to me and ask

is that creativity you display, in that time old-classy way
that of the late Billie Holiday?
For my rendition of the blues, has left the universe
without another soul to fill my shoes.

As an African-American, it has been instilled
young in me
that higher education is the key that sets my spirit free
In 1862, I was the first Black woman
to receive a B.A. degree
and go on to become a teacher and role model for the
entire world to see
I am Mary Jane Patterson
and my accomplishments in literacy are second to none.

My life is my heritage from beginning to end
a tale so profound the human heart could never
comprehend
the library's books do not depict an accurate account
of my passage from my African home range to the
struggles of America's social change look to the soul of
a Black woman to tell it all
when the battle against oppression rose
we aided in that call...
it is there, it is here, in my struggles,
in my heart and in my prayers
that you should find the essence of me
the epitome of African-American History.

CELEBRATING US!
Marcus, Malcolm, and Martin should not die in vain
Millions of our ancestors' spirits should not drift about
the Atlantic Ocean
In vain
For they are there. They still hover over its murky
waters
Drifting about from West to east and back again
Beckoning to us for acknowledgment of their buried
existence
Their forgotten existence
The African Holocaust – 100 Million Dead – At the
bottom of the Atlantic
They are   calling   to   us children   summoning us
home to Zion
From Senegal to New Orleans, From Angola to Bahia,
From Guinea to Puerto Rico
From Sierra Leone to New York City , From St. Croix to
St. Louis, From Jamaica to Honduras,
From Trinidad to Venezuela to Houston, Texas to
Canada
-          The pulse of their mother is in the heartbeat
of her children
across the diaspora.................... Please.   do
not   be   silent
we MUST celebrate us and
rejoice in the light of the beauty of Duke Ellington and
Thelonius Monk and Charlie Parker
and the pain of Billie Holiday, Miles Davis and John
Coltrane the love of Louis Armstrong
and Sarah Vaughn and Count Basie
Learn lessons from the torment of Bojangles and Amos

and Andy
Blackface, Esther Rolle and Mam-my
Understand the pain couched within the double
consciousness
Of uncle tom Because we do wear the mask…..
we must celebrate us
loving Brown Skin and Nappy roots residing in us
through the words of
Dunbar and Hughes-Wheatley and Walker-Cullen and
Baldwin
Sanchez and Giovanni- Chesnutt and Morrison and
Hurston
Loving our rhythm and drum and bass through catalysts
like -Fela Kuti and Stevie Wonder
Biggie Smalls and Tupac Shakur - Marvin Gaye and
Donny Hathaway - Aaliyah Haughton and
Minnie Ripperton - The Last Poets and Dead Prez - The
Commodores and Black Star - Robert
Nesta Marley and Lauryn Hill - Jimmy Hendrix and
Lenny Kravitz – Earth, Wind, and Fire
and Parliament/Funkadelic And Outkast
we must celebrate us
Can you not hear Africa's rhythm through the pulse of
the youth
As you wonder what dancing has to do with it
The drum and the dance – our original communication
Talking consciousness – subconsciously as we dance
- because, within, and in spite of   our pain
Her diluted drum beat alive in Salsa and rhumba –
samba and meringue – rock and roll
Hip hop and jazz – country and the blues and soul

We must celebrate us because Black History as
American History
Yes Black History is American History. Unique is Our
Story is unique and our improvisation
abounds in the accomplishments of Albert P. Albert,
inventor of the cotton picking machine –
Nathaniel Alexander, inventor of the folding chair,
Charles M. Banks – inventor of the jack
and the hydraulic jack – William Barry, inventor of the
postal machine – David Bondu,
inventor of the golf tee – Oscar E. Brown, inventor of
the horseshoe – John Albert Burr
inventor of the lawn mower – Joseph Hunter Dickinson,
inventor of the phonograph –
Robert F. Flemmings, Jr., inventor of the guitar, Garrett
Augustus Morgan, inventor of the
traffic signal – George T. Sampson, inventor of the
clothes drier, and George Washington
Carver – inventor of paint and stain and cosmetics - And
Angela Davis, bell hooks,
Henry Louis Gates, Elijah Mohammed, His Imperial
Majesty Haile Selassie I, W.E.B. Dubois and
Booker T. Washington
Inventors of Independent Thinking Brains
Yes.
We must celebrate us
Because Marcus, Malcolm, and Martin
Did not die in vain

Chapter 3
Body & Soul

BODY SERIES PART 3
i long to slip in
between the spaces of your vertebrae
and be a soft ache
when old age comes

CELLULITE
Sell-you-light/that's right
they try to sell you lite beer/lite cake/lite cookies/
Pepsi lite/99% fat-free
but who's trying to be fat-free?
certainly not me
let me see your thighs jiggle
they're jiggling, baby
go 'head, baby

This is a poem for the fat girls like me
don't tell me I'm not fat
that's like saying I'm not Black
yes *technically* my skin is brown
but I say I'm Black because I'm
down with the Blackness
like I'm down with the fatness
because fat is health is life is fertility is womanly
let me see your belly jiggle
it's jiggling, baby
go 'head, baby

It's the way women's bodies are built—we jiggle
even really thin women jiggle a little
unless they work out to have a body of steel
but who wants to look like that? get real!
This poem is a thank you
to the big bodacious mujeres de Cuba
who taught me by example to know no shame/
show no shame
to the big body women of the West Indies
who know how to wind/wind/wind at

CHECK THE RHYME/AYA DE LEON

Carnival time/time/time
let me see your hips jiggle
they're jiggling, baby
go 'head, baby

A sick society
turns women's bodies into problems to be solved
but anorexia ain't sexier
and bulimia ain't dreamier

Therefore next time you count calories
don't forget to count the thousands of years that
women's suitors have thought that cellulite
was quite all right
and were ready to embrace abundance

So next time you're working out on your Nordic Trac
don't forget to savor the sensual feeling of sweat
sliding down the rolls in your back
and next time you're working out
in step aerobics class
don't forget to enjoy the bounce of your ass
it's jiggling, baby
go 'head, baby

Special thanks to LL Cool J for the sample
"Cellulite" has been an Off-the-Scale production

TOUCHING INTANGIBLES
Touch me
Beyond what your eyes are seeing
Hypnotize me physically
Magnetize my inner being
Quench my thirst
Satisfy my desires
Spark the match
Set me on fire
Here's my heart
Never neglect it
Hold it tight
Inspect it and affect
Always find something different to unfold
Kiss my heart
Caress my soul
Put me on a pedestal
Cherish me like gold
Fuse with me
Until we become one
Together we'll walk
And rise with the sun.

MAROYA[1]
Making woman out of cold, steel blue light
The very light that flows out of her nostrils into the night
Into the hair that starts the first female form
      The craters in her hands make for cups that mold
      the breast
      Full of warm, caramel scented milk
The first woman's heart is made with her feet
Sturdy, itchy and created to be tough and pliant
Like the fiber in an ear of corn
      Sinews the moon made with her own tresses
      Woman's heart – lunar hair
      Her eyes folded over pieces of dust, debris, and
      stone
Stone as clear and deceiving as the mist on a wave
Even seaweed dries to unrecognizable sheaths
on the sand
      As Maroya smiled and frowned on her creation
      She realized that men would fear her daughter
      Fear her for making herself re-mark/make-able
For floating like the wind
For shifting like the weed
that bears the mark
Of her soul

[1] Maroya is the Moon Goddess in Cuban Native American Mythology.

SISTA DANCA

a-five, six
a-five, six, seven, eight.

g-u-r-r-r-l
ain't that your sista over there
sli-slidin herself
like her soul done set up shop in her hips
got ants all in her coochie cutters
check check
how she pop pops
rock rocks
shock shocks all crowds
fools drool as she wiggles
they eyes & mandibles on lock
that move right there she learned on our block
she's shakin that shimmy
showin her good-n-plenty
think she gon open her box & share
i reckon them rituals just rollin all up in her
sista dancin to drums
speakin in tongues
pumpin her arms
tock tickin her waist

a sweaty twen'y
awaits.

Chapter 4
Family

FILIPINOS AND BIRDS
My grandmother never talked much
about the Japanese
or their incessant struggle
during the Japanese era.
It was a taboo, she said
for five generations in our family.

Quiet like a secret, she told me
how the sky turned bleak
and the clouds grey
from all the smoke emitted
by the guerrilla guns fired endlessly
without remorse at innocent captives.

Women whined and shed rivers of tears
on their husbands' agony and torment
in the hands of the enemy.

Violence. Torture. Killing.
Traces of blood.
Scarred hearts.
Broken dreams.
They were everywhere.

Life was never a prerogative,
food was scarce,
liberty was unknown...
at that time.

The free men would often hide
and stealthily scour for food
to feed their women and children
helplessly waiting in their hideouts.

"You are very lucky," she said as tears trickle
tenderly from her cheeks. Bitter memories long buried
into oblivion had been rekindled again.

She stood up and opened the birdcage
on the table beside me. With the fledgling
perched on her finger, she held the bird
up high and the bird swiftly flew away.
"Bittersweet hope of flight," she said softly.
Now I understand.

TOLD HER
Her father told her to bring his shoes
She did
Her father told her get him a beer
She did
Her father told her to get him his food
She did
Her father told her to make her brother's bed
She did
Her father told her who to date
She did
Her father told her to miss the prom
She did
Her father told her to forget school
She did
Her father told her who to marry
She did
Her father told her to have many children
She did
Her husband told her to get his shoes
She did
Her husband told her to get him a beer
She did
Her husband told her to get his food
She did
Her husband told her to make the children's bed
She did
Her husband told her to—
.......BANG! (gun shot)

The warden told her to close the cell door
She did.

NUYORICAN DREAMS
I stand here in New York City
Una mujer negra with Puerto Rican Dreams
My grandmother and grandfather are in heaven
Her head is on his chest
Listening to his heart beat out a content
So real
I feel it here on earth
Although I offer them blankets, warmth, gifts, love,
kisses
They need nothing where they are now
As I reach into my bag and pull out a quilt
My grandmother tells me, "Honey, we got plenty"
"But thank you anyway"
She takes it and smiles
She knows the gift is not for her
But for me
My grandfather just smiles his simple smile
He laughs joyfully at my gesture
They have it all
I am the one who takes from them
I weave their compassion and magic
Into this chilly place
This now world
I search for my abuelita y abuelito
To supply me
With my everyday gold

GROWING UP IS NOT AN OPTION
See
He's still in the single digits
and thinks the uterus is part of the rhinoceros family
I am liberated.
Feminist.
Activist.
Womban.
Mama.
I want to maintain his innocence
But I'm in no sense
Ignorant to what's to come
We laugh until our bellies are forced to see stop signs
"Caution! Adulthood enforced."
He has those eyes
Big.
Brown.
Wide.
Mine.
He likes girls.
Not women.
Not hoochies.
Not hoes.
Because… "Mama hoes are gardening tools, u know
those things u use to make sunflowers grow?"
He wants to know the qualifications for how to be
president
Not resident pimp/player/shot-caller/b-baller
He doesn't like violence (hate is a strong word)

Unless mama and daddy say "protect yourself."
He thinks you have to get into the Marines
to be a Marine Biologist
And that periods are only at the ends of sentences
And I can't stop him from growing up
Out
He's got legs as long as mine
And how do I tell him to run?
Run away from…
Racism
Sexism
Drivin'while blackism
Capitalism
Pedophilism
Niggerism
Saggy-pants-ism
Drugism
I forgot-my-culture-ism
There is no island
to send him to
He is innocent
But in no sense
Safe
From life.
But he says
"Pray Mama, cuz prayer fixes everything and God don't
make no junk."
And I tell him I believe him.

MIRRORS
Mother and daughter mirror lives lived in separate times.
She wanted to be like mama,
but there was no room for ambition and nurturing in the
same womb
so they had to fight it out
and in the end ambition won
and she watched pieces her life die
                                        one
by
                        one
by
                one
by
one day her mother spat her out the way
her father did her and his mother before
setting off the chain of recognition -
Oh, you must be her child!
You look so much like your mummie. . .
Mama was picked from Le Pearle des Antilles
and planted in the Big Apple;
still looking for her dreams,
still dreaming,
yet unable to reach past the white walls that blinded her.
She sees them in her
and
she sees them in her
and
they live as mirror images of each other
coexisting on the axis of a woman's burden -
just leave yourself behind and it will manifest itself in
your fruit,

somewhere in a better place and time.
Mama labored so that she could have peace
Peace of mind,
peace of body,
but for daughter,
only differences define that peace,
knowing
mirror images they are,
knowing
Le Pearle des Antilles
the Big Apple is not.

PAINTED SKY AGAINST ANOTHER SKY
This has been: mother's Quakers, diamond drillers,
someone was once a Union soldier.

In Red Meadows, my father fishes for trout.
I fish, too, my line catching another submerged log.

I appear like the products of white color: flour, salt,
sugar. What is most my own are things that are absent.

The color old lives in my mother's household.
She doesn't polish the furniture anymore, just the frames
holding relatives.

In bondage to the river, my father fishes for speckled
bodies. His line quivers in the wake of small fish.

I catch trees. My younger brother throws rocks.
And the photos will say *family vacation*.

BEACH FURNITURE
She was an obstacle for children carrying
wet sand back to castles, big woman
in a small beach chair.
She sat in shallow water,
heavy bottom sagging like a diaper
in the seat's bright stripes.
She was beautiful
with her eyes closed, greasy fingers stretched
on wooden arm rests.
I rubbed lotion on her back, no SPF
because she wanted to get real dark.
Her black bathing suit bulged
from all of her stuffed inside.
I traced the dimples on her thighs with my fingers.
It was the same brand of chair every summer,
something west coast like San Mar or Del Rio
and she stuck it in the sand
like saltwater taffy in teeth.
I made the tuna sandwiches
in the cooler, the ones she handed out
when the time was right
and sea gulls weren't watching.
My sister shivered, wrapped
in Holiday Inn towels under umbrella.
My mother said, "That b*tch is bound to burn
beyond recognition."
Back then I didn't know what alliteration was.

EAST ST. LOUIS
i saw you squat down, slow and grand,
gathering dusty little boys
into the billows of your skirt.
you warmed them like bread –
dabbing shortening on their faces
and coating their hands with flour.

you called to my father,
and your wiles, your wiles . . .
                              irresistible.
papa-coon,
red,
gae-gae,
junior, neicee – (your babies),
you called them
to smell the sour buttermilk of your bosom
and sample the sweet tea
that gathers in rivulets
in the crook of your arm.

your screen door is patched with wire
given to you by miss mary and
she still has your cake plate.
she sent gene to come and get it
and before he walked out, you remembered
you needed some rag bologna, souse, cheese
and crackers.
you paid him in cold pop and moon pies.

your hugs are huge monsoons
that wash over nephews
back from chicago, cleveland, detroit and

california. nappyheaded and battered.
ashamed, broke, strung-out
home to try cold turkey
and lay their cheek
against your tall chiffrobe.

you gave catnip to
all of the young mothers
to soothe their colicky babies,
and the peppermint in your purse
is a better reward than heaven.

your rough hands
can turn fat drippings to soap,
and pig snoots to haute cuisine.

you called my father catfish.
you saw how he watched *everything,*
culling the bottom,
and scribbling down the dirt
in his mind.

you told him every closed eye ain't sleep,
and you gave him a bible for graduation.
inside it, he found
a folded up five dollar bill
and a note to keep on in the name of jesus.

he put the greenback in his pocket
and turning to make sure no one was watching,
he brought the bible to his face
and inhaled.

Chapter 5
For All the Women

GIMME A BREAK
Right about now
I'mma about to take a break
for all the women in the world
who have to wear their daughters hand-me-downs
who haven't been to the restroom alone since the first
baby was born.

I am about to take an extra long shower with the door
locked , for all the sweatshop industry women
I'mma get clean for all the stripping independent
oxymoron life women
the endless hustle women
behind the glass, khakis, and cornrows women
the open acceptance of oppression women

I am taking a break
buying the $200 massage for the bad mouth women
the give natural birth women
the epidural momma who had enough of the labor
drama.

I am going to the gym
and sit in the sauna,
and not even work out
for the anorexic and bulimic women in the world.

My rest is my libation before I...
Gonna watch a marathon for the
bound feet women of the world
I'm gonna have an instant orgasm for the
mutilated women in the world

Yes, I'm gonna have a drink in the middle of the week
for the middle class women
who think oppression of women is extinct
I ain't gon' wear no bra
for all the breast cancer women
because you just don't know whatcha' had 'til it's gone.
I ain't gon' wear no clothes
so I won't have to do no more damn laundry laundry
laundry

My rest is my libation before I…
Gonna sing sing sing sing sing sing sing
to drown out all dem unwanted babies
crying because he said it was God's plan
but I'm doin' all the work
men talkin' shit about reproduction

I'm gonna take a break
for the women of the world with never ending
headaches
I'mma just BREATH
and it ain't gon' be cuz I'm mad
or trying to accept another night of marital rape
or bus stop harassment

Today I'mma just
I'mma just
be a woman
and see if Lenny really knows what that is.

I'mma just
be a woman

and watch the world fall apart if
one day we all took a week off to celebrate.

My rest is my libation before I...
for the woman race that has us tired
I'mma just take a very tiny break
and plan our revolution
Some women might have to die
because they are slowing us down
but before we decide we will need uniforms
they will be cute
   but they won't be pink
they will be fire
   but they won't be sparkly
and our revolution
   will be televised
during the game.

THE MOTHER
I AM THE MOTHER
          OF MOTHER EARTH
I AM THE MOTHER
        OF FATHER TIME
        I AM THE MOTHER
        OF THE UNIVERSE
Doe Re Me,
Do Re Me-
Do Read Me…
As every Woman
'cause All my Sisters are
All one Woman
I am Them
They are me
We are Us
Us means We
I = We.

I am what I am,
So I be how I be.

Examine,
Investigate,
Peruse thoroughly-
Take a closer look,
now what do you think
about the way you perceive
the things you see?
I am what I am,
So I be how I be.

CHECK THE RHYME/HADIYAH NICOLE GREEN

Now, if I fry my hair
and smudge my beauty in make-up,
Or my back is bare
and wear a skirt short to my butt,
Or my legs clean with Nair
with high heels and a power strut,
Or I'm too shy, too quiet to share
and I just like to keep it shut,

Or I'm elegant, regal, with my nose in the air
and I'm too good to talk, smile, or touch,
Or I rock my Afro picked with care
and I'm down for the cause like what,
Or I'm braided down looking around
for my counterpart King Tut,
Or I'm gifted packaged rare
that's a wrap – now cut,
Back to the top people

I am what I am
so I be how I be

See, all my Sisters are me
I am the Mother of society,
The Mother of Mother Earth,
The Mother of Father Time,
The Mother of the Universe,
but somewhere I lost my mind
and let my body take control,
working, jerking, and nowadays

twirking
reduced my treasure chest
to a pleasure hole
all on tv or at the party
doing wild things
I lost respect for me

I forgot my soul,
my sole purpose
how can I teach humanity
if I'm so busy twirking it?
Or what am I teaching?

Wait a minute,
what's that I see?
It's a reflection
in the mirror,
My reflection –
a reflection of me.
The Mother –

How dare me
reduce myself
to a piece of meat,
allow myself
to be a misused treat?
I hold my head down
and I look at my feet.

I look at my feet as
I walked
along the banks of

the Congo,
the Niger, and the Nile,
in the lands of Togo,
Benin, and Guinea Bissau.

I walked
along the banks of
the Amazon
and the Mississippi.
My body - sold
before I strolled,
no I ran
to what I thought was free land.

My feet have carried me
so many places,
over time I've had
so many faces,
I never wore no clothes
in the Congo,
but now
I need a replacement-
A substitute.
There is none.
Just go back to your roots,
Sankofa
– my truth.

I AM LIFE.
I GIVE LIFE.
GOD PASSES LIFE
THROUGH ME.

CHECK THE RHYME/HADIYAH NICOLE GREEN

I gave birth to civilization
therefore
all of man's creations,
A-Z,
starting with the alphabet,
no, better yet
the Hieroglyphs…
no need to continue
'cause you catch my drift.

So now I know
in between my legs
is a treasure untold,
richer than
any mine,
rarer than
any gold.
You can't understand me
because
I'm too thorough.

But one day
you will all know…
in the palm of my hands
is the entire globe,
When the wind moves
its because I blow,
When the sun shines
its because I let my light show,
And when it rains outside
its because I let my water flow
I am the queen mother

of the king
and the pharaoh.
I am so thorough.
I am the Mother
          of Mother Earth,
I am the Mother
          of Father Time,
I am the Mother
          of the Universe

But I need to
re-teach
my body
and re-train
my mind.
My soul knows
where my feet have been
My mind and body
can remember
by looking within.
'I can wade in the water'
to wash away all my sins.
I can reclaim my glory
and be born again
Without a book,
a building,
a ballot, or
a bullet.

My ship has sailed
the seas standing

the test of time as
the tide tried to turn me out
but I open my eyes
3D to see
to let my ancestors guide me
to manifest my destiny
to realize my true beauty
to understand my responsibility
to my sister's children in society
to my brother's masculinity and
to my femininity the most profound combination
but you see how they tried to play me
in the creation

But now the time
for my re-education
and when its time
disseminate the information.
Exercise the virtue of patience.
While the —isms
cause my people to awaken
I'll get my hater vaccination
because…

I AM THE MOTHER
        OF MOTHER EARTH.
I AM THE MOTHER
OF FATHER TIME.
I AM THE MOTHER
        OF THE UNIVERSE.
I AM
THE MOTHER!

SHE'S SLEEPING
I can hear the silent cries of my soul at night
Wishing change would come
So I could take flight
Nature of a woman I cannot define
A definition of me can only come from my mind
Seasons strange, babies came and I am not to blame
Control of the heavens by creating the stars
Born to shoot, but really how far?
Look at my reflection
Who do you see?
I am a woman that lives and bleeds
Focus is a virtue, liberty is a statue
Land of the free, and home to my mother
I'm walking in the shadows of my fathers and brother
No force could rest with this fate
Femme fatale, blessed as the bait
You took it, hook, line and sinker
In the heat of passion I became the thinker
I tinkered with boys' toys
And took a moment to understand
Why I was born a woman, and he was born a man
Do you ever wonder what it's like to be me?
Don't trip
I'm not talking simple sexuality

I am walking in the shadows of shadows
But the light is coming soon...

Dimmed dawns, loves lost
I yawn, gender holocaust
Tired of the role

I'm crying because she's dying
But don't bother to console
I can tolerate the ups and downs from love to hate
Through dark alleys I walk at night alone
Sometimes lonely but mostly at home
Street lamps like a mother's embrace
I can feel her touch, can't remember her face
She cries in silence
A moment from time capsules of ages past
I recognize with these eyes that I am not the first

Nor will I be the last
Woman, flexible to change
Feminine to masculine, I can rearrange
Falling into the reality of where I stand
I was born a woman, and he was born a man

Innocent, smelled on the breath of an infant
Direct descendant, of eye and I
I deny all laws of gravity with unknown ability I fly
High in thought is how I get high
Universes dispersed in the abyss of my uterus
I am a GOD, anonymous

I am walking in the shadows of shadows
But the light is coming soon
We have seen the strength of the sun
Through reflections of the moon

I look back, I look back, and again I look back
Warmed by the fires of my desire

CHECK THE RHYME/THAILAN NGUYEN

To the point of melting
Consumed until I heard the last bell ring
Saved by it, once a slave but I defy it
Words connect, time project, God is erect
From blue depths of her sky
In the moment, so why try and cry?
By words alone we cannot be defined
Like birds we roam in the open night sky
Spiraling through movement of the pendulum
Fluid formations, do you remember them?
Patterns played through his vision
Without her essence there was a division
Of the voice to the sound
The choice to be bound...or free
It takes more than one to achieve unity

She is flying in the shadows of shadows
But the light is coming soon...
I had a dream tonight
There was a moonbow at the peak of my flight.

WHEN HE DEMANDS ALL MY POEMS
BE WRITTEN TO LIBERATE BLACK AMERICA
i tell him i can see the intricacies
between mental health and
black liberation struggle
the slow deaths and slow suicides
turned in over and onto themselves
due to a wounded black psyche
crippled by capitalist and colonial america.

what black woman can livvvvve
without first giving voice
to Her pain.
brother don't you know
that sistah's cannot heal
until we first testify

cuz healing and testimony
are intertwined
and black women will *always*
be heard
humming in the night.

call me daughter of the dust
mother to eve
sister to Yemanja
and cousin to Oshun

resisting the currents
of your nationalist politics and
limited sexist mind

trying to put a chokehold
on the human heart
that cannot be contained

or confined
in your little bitty ole box
that seeks to silence
and keep black women
objectified.

every time i feel the need
i give myself permission
to cry.

to shake loose the shoulds
and extreme corporeality
attached to my
beautiful black skin.

to run wild with the werewolves
my spirit-consciousness
rising and ascending
inward toward wholeness
where i make continual pilgrimage
to me . . . .

once i was mute
but today i'm gonna give myself
validation
to spread my wings
and resurrect the old bones
of my ancestors

once buried at the bottom
of some wide sargasso sea

so gather up your sounds
and listen
to this fierce indomitable
black woman speak
about loneliness depression and anxiety.

cuz the reality is not only mine.

i'm here to tell you:
"the strong black woman has died."
and i can hear ntozake shange sayin
this is a poem for colored girls
who have considered suicide
when the niggers were too afraid to kill.

i seek solace in sanchez's haiku

know full well that *"i am"*
not only fire but also earth
air & water too.

and some say
"phillis wheatley never sang the blues"
when she was ripped and torn
from her mother/land.

even nella larsen weeped
cuz she was tired of passin
and sick of sinkin in her own quicksand.

yeh. proof enough.
that consciousness precedes

what may look like a problem to you.
baby. even aretha franklin knew
that she couldn't become conscious
until she first articulated
freein herself from a chain of fools.

in my world the Higher mind rules
over militant blk/rhetoric
absent of love or truth.

i'm not sayin i'm givin credence
to victimhood or 'woe is me'
cuz i resist victimhood
and codependency.

but i will work at expressing
the *totality* of my being.
because i know that
in order to fully liberate
black america
i must first heal
unconditionally love
honor
and cherish me.

Chapter 6
Growing Up in the 'Hood

STREET/ANGELS
half burned structures
of usta be buildings
stand uninhabitable
with jagged/glass-etched windows
that frame the faces
of children/looking for a place
to hide/a refuge from the streets/where
rage is a weapon.
fueled by the insatiable hunger
that poverty creates/we are
all prisoners/detained
within a 5 mile radius
we become each other's targets...
mothers.
dark girls
strolling with peppermint breath
and pickles
walking with misconceived notions
of womanhood/they greet disappointment
warmly laugh when misery
comes to court.
black and blue mamas
that never call their babies in
look past crevices
that seal secrets
that shoulda been told
while procreation feeds madly
at the breasts of young girls
unaware

of the Sun.
mother's young men
stalking night creatures
alone on crowded streets
dance with death.
twisted warriors
beat each other/instead of the drum
the seeds of griots, prayer kings
and medicine men
have forgotten ceremony.
in the new-jack village
men-children
dance on junkie piss
with long muscular strides
they cruise defeat
never knowing
that they can fly.
mother father/mother
help Mary
mother of God's
motherless children
whose screams silently fill
empty rooms
broken Angels
that wear the stench
of other people's sins
grieve prematurely
  nobody must know
    i can't tell/nobody

what they do to me/i can't tell
  what they do to me
babies that never learn to smile
  i can't tell
who will hold the hopeless
  i can't tell
  what they do to me
mother pray for us/mother guide us
when we don't know
what we do/mother forgive us
when we do what we know/mother
i have seen you cry
in a day-old-dress
with a bottle of gin
you were clinging
to passing promises/Mother
open our eyes
that we
may see You in We
and Love
Us unconditionally.

NO WHERE BUT HERE

No where but here are we living sitting in the midst of a
dream.
BROKEN
Here, they sell that watered down fragrance at the GAP
And label that shit Dream.
Come visit my stomping grounds
And I'll show you survival.
Dogding heat packing brothers
And shorties with quick tongues
Who threw disses or spit blades
That left a crescent across your face.
A Buck 50
Taped up
Shaped up
Bopping through the Streets
With the crew all dipped up.
While poverty
Was just a state of mind
That TV forced
Down our throats
Like Nyquil
But only
Worse.
Said we was deprived.
Neglected.
And rejected.
we held on to our disabilities
and flipped it into Spanglish.
From BK to el barrio,
From the Iowa deck, to soundview.
To every tecato street thug, named Papo.
Here.

BIRDS
For my birds
In concrete jungles
Sitting on branches
Of organized bureaucracy
Watching the asphalt grow
Creating new crimes
To fill new prisons
For my little birds
Named children of despair
Sitting on trees growing
Under paper moons
And frozen rainbows
Hopscotch and double-dutch on
Playgrounds of unborn dreams
Hope never flies
With clipped wings
Poverty is their toy
For my caged birds
Who still sing
Would be leaders
Showing courage behind bars
Teaching new songs to
Untapped spirits hidden under
Jerseys and ball caps
Making street corner wishes
On Genies in Hennessy bottles
Trying to make a dollar
Out of what makes sense
For my birds

CHECK THE RHYME/MIKAYLAH SIMONE

Faith lies in dime bags as
Turning Virgin Mary's
Last name to "Jane"
Getting religion from television
Praying to an altar of cable gods
With benevolent offerings
Of robot souls
…This is for my birds

COMMON KNOWLEDGE
It's common knowledge
we hood girls don't cry.
We were born without tear ducts.
We're not even fully human.
Two hearts full of anger and faceless passion,
and half a brain,
kelvins in our veins.
That's why we thrive in the Coldest Winter.

If ever we were more than orifices
to pleasure multiple men
in singlets, couplets, and etc., etc.,
it was in prehistory
before the written word
it's common knowledge.

We are descended directly from
slave chattel raped senselessly into submission-
Hottentot was our foremother-
we rage against our roots,
thinking we do what is pleasurable,
unwittingly looping history into present times.

If ever a hood girl was to cry,
through absent tear-ducts,
that moisture would pollute the ground,
and is generally considered unworthy of comment.

It is common knowledge
that God loves all His Creation,
man, and beast, fish and fowl alike,
and God collects the tears of his beloved children

into gold-and-sapphire challices.
Then angels fashion each individual tear
into a hymn so replete with glory
the sun awakens from his slumber to hear the sound.

It's common knowledge, however,
that the hood girl, our genus unknown,
our pedigree dubious,
is altogether undeserving of such tribute.
So our tears, scantily falling though they may be,
serve as nothing more than water for the weeds.

Chapter 7
Haiku

CITYSCAPE HAIKU #1
sun forms crystal rays
against the syringe on my step
as I seek the day

CITYSCAPE HAIKU #2
your hands touch vinyl
a circular odyssey
culminates my love

CITYSCAPE HAIKU #3
coral blue green caps
paraphernalia rainbows
city birdseed feast

PRAISE HAIKU
sucked in or poked out
muscular soft flat or round
woman love your belly

Chapter 8
Identity & the Mirror of Self

PRESSURE MIX
I am Mountain rich as coal
Pressed, condensed
To make diamonds and gold
(these, my friend, I give to you, to the end)
"What are you?" he asks
"What are you?" she asks
"Where are you from?" they ask
If you do not recognize it
It's because you've been taught
To separate and categorize it
My toes which can climb
And balance on slivers
Are the Andes
And its flowing rivers
My arches, thick ankles and calves
Have seen many things
That you have
They've pushed and carried
Under the overlord's strain
And crouched and huddled
Under rubber trees in the rain
But they've also done a skank
To Bad Brains
And stepped to the soulful sounds
of "Love Train"
My stomach is tense with the
Spanish explorer's fear he will fail
But it has also eaten the slave's slop
from a pail

My lungs have breathed the guava-scented
Air of the Caribbean shore
And the *Zimne Piwo* and Polish sausage
Of Chicago's Northwest Side stores
My dark eyes began under the
Middle-eastern sun
And rested under the moon of
Guyana, when the day was done
My skin is scars that heal light,
Like the person who inflicted the wound
And scars that heal dark,
Like the person who received it.
I am the mouth of the liar
Who will always lie
And the ears of the fool
Who will always believe it.
My hair is the dry Sahara
My nails, Lake Michigan freshwater pearls
My interior is masculine fury
My form is a fragile girl
My spirit, the careless order of the housewife
And the feigned concern of the house servant,
The decadence of the media mogul
And the loving acceptance of the small merchant
My blood is light and dark and red
Acid and base
Neutralized in my flesh
My heart is tough

Midwestern beef jerky
And thin, Japanese seaweed
My soul, the madness of a dogbite
And the soft, newborn child's need
I am the hated and loved
The feared and revered
That indefinable, high-yellow-mulatta-trigena-mixed-
something-or-other
No one wants to go near
Called stupid, sleazy, crazy
Conceited and a shame
Not trusted, not understood
Not forgiven, and always blamed
What are you afraid of? That I am master and servant in
one?
That I am rich and poor in one? That I understand both?
That I do not fit into your categories? That I know no
one has ever fit into them?
I am that person you dare dismiss
With "What ARE you?"
LOOK at me!
I am the same as you!
I am family
I have lived in your home
Walked your continents
Crossed your oceans
Loved your loves
Lived your lives
And cried your cries

CHECK THE RHYME/GRISEL ACOSTA

What *am* I?
I am.
I am here.
I am yours.
And you are mine.
We are each other's,
FOREVER.

INNOCENCE

Innocence is my witness.
She is there most every time.
I need her presence to grip with.
As we look at the scene of the crime.

She's so very strong.
I feel almost weightless.
She carries a light to see the wrong.
We wonder who created this.

A hole that is wide and deep,
dark and deserted.
Slowly we creep,
hoping no one will hurt us.

We examine the evidence,
wanting enough to build a case.
I am not a party to this pretense
and feel no need to erase my face.

How will they set me up,
with the cracks in the walls?
Like an army they hup
and measure my falls.

The time cuts through me.
Blood splatters to the floor.
Innocence moves inside me,
and begins healing my sore.

Her light shinning within me,

my own fading faster.
the hope she has given me,
builds my character.

I must be strong.
She will see to it.
No matter how long.
We will go through it.

CLARITY
i am looking for
clarity
have you seen her?
the last time i saw her she told me of the time
she was robbed said she was little
and no one heard her screaming/said someone
took her innocence and she needs it back.
i am looking for clarity
have you seen her?
the last time i saw her
she was grieving under
a lamp post wondering where her mind had gone/said
she didn't know when she had it last
but is worried because she is hungry
and can not recall if
anyone loves her
enough to feed her
i am looking for clarity
have you seen her?
the last time i saw her
she was bent
over dirty syringes and maddog labels
she was
giving her ass up
for a shot of whiskey
and a cigarette/i
am looking for clarity
i heard that she has AIDS

and roams the streets
smoking cigarettes/holding
an empty flask
looking for the place
they told her to go
for the free cab/to
the free food at/the free
clinic where no one
knows her name and
certainly no one
understands that
nothing
in
clarity's life
is free.
i am looking for clarity i cannot find her
i am afraid that she is somewhere screaming
and no one hears her/i am afraid that the only thing
clarity hears is the sound of her own voice
ringing/screaming
between her ears
because
somethings
in life
are unavoidably
clear.

THAT GIRL
I am no longer that girl. That girl was a buck, she rode
devils, she wore short skirts that showed some thigh, too
much, she played ditch, double trouble, skipped double
dutch.

> She did him wrong and her best friend wrong
> and her mama wrong. She wore tight shirts that
> showed off small breasts, she was country.

She was treeless branches, drank gin and Miller High
Life, and she shook her hips like this and she shook her
hips like that. She was the black bird and the sun.

> She spoke woman tongue. She crawled till she
> had grass stains melt on her belly. She took her
> first curve fast, she was a fast talker, she wore
> bells, drank her thick coffee brown.

She played the afternoon like it was her boyfriend
coming home. She called him sweet sunshine, rain,
called him up one way and down another.

> Boyfriend! Called him baby cakes, honey bun,
> angel, she called, her high voice high, loud. She
> was the afternoon, the town store that sold
> pecans and sugar sticks, wore her uncle's
> cowboy hat, spit tobacco.

She was the picnic and the quilt spread lazily on the bed. She was all legs spread on the box spring when she made love.

> She was the stone he threw in the creekbed. She was bed post and her mama's best helper. She was Turtle Road, Holy Cross Church, and the Cash Variety store.

She was every road that led her. She was Home.

PETALS OF DANGER
poison perfume
thorny handfuls
of hormones
and mousse
M.A.C. truck lips
Rock Star breath
jockey for position
in mirrors
and hearts

MASQUERADE
(Inspired by Nikki Giovanni)
I'm fading
Praying someone will find me
Disguised behind painted on
portraits of perfection
We wear the masks
Behind your erections
convinced that perfection
can be improved upon
born of love, ripped from man's side
to bring back balance
Masquerading behind mascara
and lipstick smeared mistakes
we've forgotten what the truth looks like
hiding behind the superficial masks we create
searching our own reflections
for something real
beyond manufactured smiles
painted over
broke hearts
and lost souls
trying to conceal
loose teardrops for fear of finding something real
Don't look now
I'm fading
Away
Don't look now
I'm fading
Fading

into this faceless fortress
a forgotten self
wearing black and blue
like it's the new you
dress yourself in a lie
and pretend that its true
but real beauty
is in the eyes of the beholder
somebody just needs to hold
her keep her
from falling
Slipping into the abyss of
society
vanishing
and the spotlight is blinding
we spend so much time
hiding
behind
this illusion like
Carbon copied teardrops
Falling in line
like all of societies other clones
stripped of self
and left alone
stripped of self
and left
alone
stripped of self

and left
alone
here I am
I'm fading
Away
Here I am
I'm fading
Disappearing in the distance
They say it's a matter of perception
But society says so
So we erase individuality
And make the correction
We wear the masks of deception
Stripping away
Self love;
Baby girl
Don't you know can't
nobody else love you,
Unless you love you
And everything underneath
The mask

MUSING
A woman looking at me, gazing, staring
Hair mingling with her smile like old friends chatting,
Perhaps i should have gone natural,
Perhaps i should have married JC,
Time would have taught me to love him
Perhaps i should have dreamed less,
Turned my back on me, succumbing to kindred cries
Perhaps i should have dreamed less.
As the woman reflects regret in her image's mirage,
One morning, reaching to touch forty and its dazzling
likeness,
She sees remorse disappear in her sunset's bloom.

MY TEMPLE IN THE CITY
If I left now would it be difficult to return
To the same place in which I stood before the world
turned?
Cannot stop time, I know this
It's like laughter
God will provide the bookmark of life after I've lived
the final chapter
Life goes too fast for me to reminisce the past
Names and numbers too many for me to memorize and
do the proper math
I have a concern that I just can't shake
It hits my mind once again as soon as I awake
I don't know what it is
I can't describe it
It's got a distinct feel though so I like to fall asleep
beside it
I read a book and it asked me
What do I want out of life?
I wanna be healthy so why not happy
And so I set my sights…
How many songs have I sang that mean the exact same
thing
Will there come a day when I'll renounce everything I
used to think
Does it matter?
Avoiding apathy by crowding my thoughts with pop
scatter
The best view of Manhattan is from Brooklyn
May just be my perspective but trust me
I've been looking
From many points of the city
It's happening and so a million fish will bite

One by one we're hooked in the shallow waters of a
meaningful life
And in the night
Can you remember your dreams?
I can't say which is better
Depends on what you see
And you can find the same teller on St. Marks
But I can't promise you that she'll recognize you after
dark
If it's in the control of your mind then what are you
waiting for?
If it's written on your palm then you are destined for
more…

MS. DANDELION
I never promised you a rose garden
and I am not a rose
not a posh and spoiled flower
raised in velvet soil pampered by a gardener's touch
I am a dandelion
blossoming between cracks in pavement
I make ghetto gardens beautiful
where neglect has run rampant
petals like slivers of sunshine
young girls braid me in their hair
they know I am glorious
organic gold
my crown is their crown
making queens out of girls with ashy knees
and gap-toothed grins
my children float on air like
warm snow in August
populating the globe with my essence
my face is world-renowned
In France they call me the tooth of the lion
dente de lion
finding ferociousness
in my jagged green leaves...
No, I am not your common
garden-variety rose
cut down and destroyed by every
Tom, Dick and Harry of a virus
coddled by particular human hands...
I am a dignified weed
from the garden of a princess
to tha projects

cut down by shears
torn up by the roots
trampled by the bottoms of soiled air-force ones
I grow again

I am the lion's tooth
I refuse to be conquered
I am a dandelion.

THAT TWINBROOK TIGER
In D.C. my classmates knew I was half
black. There were others like me, darker
than me.
I had a different last name
than my sister.
Same eyes, same mother.

I'm still searching for something that tastes
like the almost all soy burgers I waited in
line for behind blue-black
little girls with greasy braids. I was jealous of

their beads, the big round ones, bulbous
and bright on elastics wrapped around
the ends. They looked like gumballs I wasn't allowed to
have.

Chapter 9
I Dream of Hip Hop

MIDDLE PASSAGE
15th Century
sharks tried to capture our undeveloped hips curving
around pen-tips
the ocean floor tried to steal our soul(s)
the atlantic tried to mimic our indigenous phonemes
wrapped around
breaths that tagged west africa's wind-
they did not succeed

21st Century
mics provoke us
five elements devour us
black gyrl spoken word
patois of the urban terrain
demystified boisterous tongues-
demanding to be heard

we are the un*monolithic* reincarnated hip hop generation
of female fetuses
tossed overboard

BUILT TO LAST
As a kid, I thought I couldn't be an emcee
cuz I was a girl
and so nobody encouraged me
All those years I held back, what a shame
hip hop slipping down the drain
I sat on sidelines and complained
waiting in vain
instead of using my brain
I had nothing to lose
and everything to gain
but female conditioning conditioned me to wait
I checked my calendar, my watch
that shit was ten years late
cuz it was my voice
that I was longing to hear
I got a lot to say
come near & open your ears

I'm not a pimp
I'm not a hoe
I'm not a slanger or a noc
I probably won't get any respect
if I roll up on your block
but I respect myself
enough to tell the truth
not play some gangster role
just to impress the youth
it's uncouth and unethical
instead I practice breath control
work with young people and I try to make them skeptical
don't believe all that you see on TV

every gold tooth emcee ain't got a ghetto pedigree
stop fronting, start hunting for your true identity
cuz the hip hop community gots mad diversity
bring authenticity that people can feel
I don't conceal I will reveal and this is how I keep it real
real hair real nails real tits real ass
real smart real age and I'm built to last...

FLASHING TRIBUTE
for grandmaster flash and jazzy joyce

Here's the remedy for your chronic whiplash

   Coming to you via triple ones on a mission

Pop a wheelie for originators of the flash

Check ya dial, emboss the rock b4 a fella dip dash

Grand sure slammed a party – peep two needles in collision

   Here's the remedy for your chronic whiplash

Flare your dome w/ a pinch of cheeba cheeba succotash

   Got my avenue peaking from rapid circumcision

Pop a wheelie for originators of the flash

Ululate the call; gods never caught tongue-lash

   Tweak an eq before Jazzy sparks double vision

   Here's the remedy for your chronic whiplash

Got my tambourine for ya partner now pass the calabash

Smile for the DJ when the cut spits – peep the precision

Pop a wheelie for originators of the flash

Never fret what the beat can establish from the trash

Master meter on Orion, starship blast w/ supervision

Here's the remedy for your chronic whiplash

Pop a wheelie for originators of the flash

FANTASTIC FEMME POETIC HIP HOP ANTHEM

I'm not your ho
I won't flip my skirt for you
I won't lose my worth for you

I won't give you my
magnificentwomanpoeticpower
because you don't understand the
stride in my step
and the strength of my spirit

Go on girl!

I'm not your skeez
I won't get down on my knees and please
you bore me with your shallow needs to -
control me
choke hold me
abuse me
invalidate me
use me

I am done being pimped!
Now you're trying to take over
trying to seem important
in yo' big platinum chains
and your big range rovers

CHECK THE RHYME/DuEwa Frazier

You expect me to salivate
because all of your pride
you ate
when you signed a record deal
big money thrill
now you want to kill the love
I have for me and mine –
n**ga please!

I thought we were done
being n**gas
being sold to the highest bidder

You don't think I'm a winner
or your supa-dupa counterpart
'cause you want to take my parts
apart!

Put me up on stage
rap out all your rage
'cause you think the material
is really your identity

I'm your one and only
but you constantly loathe me
when you set a standard
that I can only
work in your industry

CHECK THE RHYME/DUEWA FRAZIER

and make top dollar
by taking off my clothes
rubbing my African body
all over you
and your boys

Look back into our legacy
I remember the original rap dynasty
the Kings and Queens
who gave us
rhyme, rhythm, wisdom
AND made the cash —

KRS, MC Lyte, Sugar Hill Gang,
Eric B. & Rakim, Grandmaster Flash,
Public Enemy and MC Shan

You act like a boy instead of a man
you need a rites of passage
and a new plan
to teach you to be more spiritual
to live with integrity
instead of pimping your counterpart — me

I look to you to be my reflection
and although I have my own mind

CHECK THE RHYME/DuEwa Frazier

I always thought that you were divine
the perfect testosterone bass
to my estrogen rhyme

But I won't bow down anymore
as long as you treat me as a whore
instead of your sister
your mate
your teacher

I will reach a brighter star
when you are ready
to be your true self
find me
whether I'm near
or far

But not a day more
will you come to my door
requesting me to bare
my brown, beautiful
sensual all
-not for a few dollars
or even a little more

*previously published in *Stardust Tracks on a Road* (Lit Noire Publishing)

BIRTH NAME

1.
I am the first voice of hip-hop
born out of a necessity to free myself
from the noose of censorship.

I was conceived in a field of cotton on a
sun-drenched porch with collards as my
sidekick.

I came of age during a time of the world's
own self discovery, when consciousness
meant opening your eyes, ears/
raising your voice—your fist.

I was first known as the slave story—
oral history. Before I could
write or read, I would listen.

With this, I would send years of tradition
to a country, a place known as free
so that one day I would grow up and
folks would call me — Poetry.

Birth father—Jupiter Hammon
my mother—first name Phillis
last name Wheatley.

She felt me.
I felt her.
She called.
I answered.

With rapping
beat boxing
spitting
rhyming
& hip-hop

the industry still has not stopped to
recognize me as the foundation
and the essence of all they compose.

I have saved souls
gave birth to those.

I suppose one day, I will reinvent
myself as myself.

This time unveiling all
that I am so there will be no
mistaken identity.

People will finally recognize me.
As I state my name proudly, loudly
as if in church on Easter Sunday Morning.

I am the first voice of hip-hop
make folks decipher while battling in ciphers;
reconsider their word choices
change their lyrical devices
drop lines
blow minds

kick beats
rule streets.

When folks see me, they speak.

2.
I rhyme like Missy
but in my eyes, I favor my aunt Gwendolyn.

My tone resembles that of my cousin Nikki
but my lips look and form like those of Lauryn.

My pitch resounds like Jill
but she inherited it from her grandmother Sonia.

My beats and rhymes sound like Common,
Kanye and 50
but they hung out all night with their
favorite uncles
T La Rock, Kool Moe Dee, Kurtis Blow,
and Eazy E.

My voice has never stopped
It will speak, sing, rap, rhyme, spit that,
beat-box and hip-hop on
until ears fall deaf
minds grow weary
words stop flowing or God stops speaking.

3.
I am the first voice of hip-hop.

I am the first voice of hip-hop.
I am the first voice of hip-hop.
I am the first voice—

and I sound like, like—
                    Poetry.

THUGLUCIOUS

(for all my brothers who live for hip-hop, instead of die for it)
thuglucious,
you be the spicy sweet i need on bitter days,
thick, rich and creamy;
from bewitched midnight to aurora's light;
corn rowed, afroed, bald and bold,
or knotty dread.
you be my inspiration wet on dry days,
hot and weathered in this desert
drenched with my ancestors' angst.
thuglucious be that heat
against the cold of ages
trying to stiffen my bones
and make a maiden old
before her time.
you be the rhyme
of ancestral dreams refined,
rhythm beating NowTime,
aria of unsung heroes and sheroes
whose names we don't know.
you be their cries beneath holocaust skies
scorching the land where we live.
you be the give
in the rope
tightened round my throat.
thuglucious,
you be the fruit falling

from the seed of unspeakable sins
redeemed.
rise ye righteous and conscious
in the wake of exalted tomorrows,
in the face of today's mighty sorrows!
you be divine;
know it is your time.
you be the rhyme
of ancestral dreams redefined.
rise ye righteous!
rise ye conscious,
and live instead of die for it,
dance instead of fight for it!
thuglucious, who you be
thuglucious, what we need
thuglucious, set us free...

MR. HIP HOP

I wanna know what's inside
Inside of
That other ride
Through the timeless mind
The kind of dream that means you're alive ride
Willing to survive and thrive inspite of the negative
vibes ride
See-
He's selling dreams for a dime
One dime at a time
A rhyme without mind
Without thought of the divine
A straight chaser losing his shine
Forgetting how to lyrically climb
The mountain inside of his own mind
His empty rhetoric is hungry for respect
While his dialect
Loses effect
To stir the intellect
'cause
He's locked in a box
Filled with heavy diamonds and rocks
At the bottom of the ocean
Moving backwards in slow motion
To keep chase
Keep pace
All the while
Wearing white face

He's locked away like a misfit
Wearing chains that disguise

The craze in his eyes!
I'm talking about Mr. Hip Hop
And the way he's closed shop
'cause money and fame
Mean more
Than lyrical props

Chapter 10
Jazz Journey

MY FATHER WAS A CATHOLIC JAZZ MUSICIAN
Say one Our Father, two Hail Marys,
and listen to twelve recordings
of John Coltrane.
Dip your fingers in the font of holy water,
cross yourself,
make your way to a pew,
genuflect, take your seat,
and meditate
on the perfection of Thelonious' chords.
For a confirmation name, you have some choices:
Ornette; Dizzy; Django; Duke; or Miles.
We will set a sign
 and a seal upon your forehead
of a saxophone,
communion
is the reed between your lips.

JUST JAZZ
You ever ride?
You ever ride on a *"Train"* for *"Miles"*
until you got *"Dizzy?"*
Got so dizzy it felt like you could fly?
Fly like a *"Bird"* man
fly so high and so close to heaven
you felt Godly like
you was the *"Monk"* of melody
the minister of music
serenading sermons of soul
into some righteous rhythms?
You ever hear?
You ever hear, then listen
to the lyrical libations of *"Louie?"*
You ever shout salvation
while *"Sachmo"* blows into your being
narrating notes of rhapsodies
into rhythms of royalty
making you feel as if you were
a King, a Queen
the *"Count"* of *"Basie"*
the *"Duke"* of *"Ellington"*
or just some beautiful *"Lady* of the *Day."*
You ever stomp your feet to the soulful sounds of
sistah *"Shara,"* sistah *"Ella"*
as they filled your sorry soul with joy
Or snap your fingers to the music of brother *"Tyner"*
You know the original, the real *"McCoy?"*

You ever jump on a jazz note and ride the rhythm?
you ever jump on a jazz note and just ride the rhythm?
Ride so far and fast
you felt compelled
to never come back.
You ever slip inside of a sax
hover under a horn
peel off a piano
or
float on a flute
until you felt like a drum?
A drum beating
into the soul of the universe.
You ever jazz man?
you ever jazz?
you ever-just jazz?

BLACKBERRY MOLASSES
Souls blend like blackberry molasses
Masses of cloudless energy play songs in one key
Something major
Something minor
They're playing
jazz in heaven
They're playing jazz in heaven
I'm writing and writing and writing and writing
Balancing between wide open spaces
Faces are blurry and features are one color
Spirits cast shadows like light
Chasing truth
Sojourning in heaven
They're saving souls in heaven
I'm physically here but my mind is soaring on the wing
of an eagle
I'm talking to angels
I'm talking to angels
I'm writing and writing and writing and writing
Balancing between wide open spaces
Faces are blurry and features are one color
Ancestors light fires
They're waking new souls in heaven
They're digging freedom tunnels in heaven
I'm physically here but my mind is walking through
thought
I'm looking for messiahs
I'm talking to unborn babies
I'm talking to unborn babies

Souls blend like blackberry molasses
Masses of cloudless energy play songs in one key
Something major
Something minor
They're playing jazz in heaven
They're playing jazz in heaven

Chapter 11
Longing & Memories of Love

SIMPLY YOU
There is a peace within
when near you that cannot be explained
Allowing all cares and frustrations to just float away
Nothing had been able to instill such feelings
That is, nothing until you

There have been years of built up pain and anguish
That have only hardened this heart and made it so cold
There were times happiness seemed so far out of reach
That is, till you placed it in my hands.

Thoughts of unworthiness constantly flooded the mind
Allowing it to believe that no good
would ever come my way
All seemed hopeless, all seemed pointless
That is, till you planted more pleasant thoughts.

When it was believed that no one else cared
People drifted away or forgot my existence
Family broke my heart time and time again
That is, till you showed me what caring really meant.

Now there are new thoughts that crowd the mind
The pain inside is slowly beginning to die
Hope again has shined it's light
That is, now that I am blessed to have you in my life.

WISH

I was beautiful today
but you weren't here to notice.
And if you had been,
my beauty likely would have gone
unremarked.
Just like my birthday,
or the changing season,
or the miles of wire
barbed with pride
that now extend
between us.

I was brilliant the other afternoon;
words fell wryly from my lips,
and subtle wit glanced the ears
of those gathered around me.
But your hooded eyes
were never dazzled by the way
my mind can shine,
and in your ears my tongue was always
too sharp, too loose, too used
to having its own way
in the world.

I was melancholy this morning.
My heart felt dull as the pewter sky
and colder than its rain.
I walked alone beneath a canopy
dimly lit by yellow leaves,
my fingers fondling empty air
instead of your warm palm.

And I missed you
though I knew
that had you been there,
your pace would have outstripped mine,
and you wouldn't have seen my misery,
being colorblind to blue.

How is it then
that I still yearn for the smell
and feel of your sweatdamp clothes,
being clutched to your chest
in a too tight embrace?
Why should I miss your sullen stare,
or strain my memory to recall the smile
so rarely won by me?
Why do I miss the hand
that never signed a card
"with love,"
or presented a bouquet of pink lilies
just because…

Perhaps it is only
the deception of this season:
dying leaves robust with color,
cold air clean with the smell of rot.

Perhaps in time
you will lose your shine,
lie unspent and tarnished
like lesser coins tossed
before the fountain ran dry.

UNTITLED
you are a strange bird
too lovely to make mine
too free to call down
from the wide open sky

yet I would still be yours
the bird sure in your palm
a soft, shuddering sparrow
with no gift but a song

DANCIN AT THE PRINTZ GRILLE
(*Wilmington, Delaware*)
Israel just got out of Rikers Island,
Wearin' a cross around his neck.
"God is the only man I fear," he says,
Throwin' up his Brooklyn sign
Wantin' me to be his savior
Lead him to eternity.
"Be my lady,
Have my babies."
"Brother, you don't even know me."
"But I like what I see."
We dance and flirt with a dream—
Stompin' out the blues at the Printz Grille.
I want to pick him up
Dust him off,
Give him the Fruit of Islam.
The Egyptian sun rises in this Brooklyn Prince.
He's not the gangsta he pretends to be.
His smile gives him away.
His eyes dance hope
Across my body.

HAIKU FOR THE REV-(S)-OLUTION
Freedom don't come for
No sleepers, ride out and drink
Plenty of Red Bull
Freedom of speech means
We should be able to use
Our cell phones no charge
Yes Brother (a song)

Yes brother I do love you

I swear I want this all
Our love can conquer mountains
With Jah we can't go wrong
Your teachings are a blessing
Each night for you I pray
One day we'll see the chapel
If asked 'till then I'll say

Chorus:
I don't fear love no more
I don't fear love no more
I don't fear – I don't fear – I don't fear
Love no more

Yes brother I do love you

I swear this won't go wrong
'till death my heart will keep you
my life is where you belong

Yes brother I adore you
For that you can be sure
It was fear that kept me distant
But I don't fear love no more

Chorus:

I don't fear love no more
I don't fear love no more
I don't fear – I don't fear – I don't fear
Love no more

*Song can be found on "Get Familiar" the double album released by Queen
Sheba in 2005

Chapter 12
Performing Poetry & Praising Poets

BREAD & WINE
this morning I had coffee with Sanchez and Sandburg
while watching the sunrise over sonnets similes sonkus
and stanzas
we savored every word like rosemary on fresh salmon
with a special surprise serving of Shakespeare's spirit

I lunched this afternoon with Lourde, Lawrence and
Locke
we laughed between incremental repetitious layers of
lyrical lines of language lady love sang a song in
Spanish soprano for Lorca it was a lyrical ballad

this evening I dined with Dylan, Dickinson
and Dante we danced while defining what it means to
be a writer by offering dramatic monologues
dinner was lengthy

I indulged myself in a nightcap with Nikki
she was the only one I called by her first name
she told me that I could
she read me to sleep as the night became the dawn
the dawn daybreak

I yawned and said *good morning* once again to them all
offering to pick up the tab on today's food for their souls
not having enough money to cover myself
sacrifice is an honor and the least that I can do for them
besides yesterdays' meal is still with me
because of them today I can fast

SLAM JAM!
Take a chance
Let your heart prance
To my serenade sashay
You haven't wept yet
So take a whiff
Of this literary bliss
Amiss from your bones
Though your soul knows the secret;
Peep it…
Stomp your feet
To this meter creep
And watch this imagery breathe
As I rhyme reach
Preach and teach
SLAM! JAM!
SLAM! JAM!
This rhythm romp, Beat stomp
Makes you bleed and sweat
metaphor pirouettes
Spinning faster and faster
Faster and faster
than your mind can even believe
rhythm wrap, simile snap
soul shimmy down to your knees
assonance slides
makes your whole body ride
a soul roller coaster
reaching closer
to where it aches

and quakes thunder
hearts asunder
take a passion plunge
alliteration lunge
into this tongue I speak
and drown.
Are you down?
SLAM! JAM!
SLAM! JAM!
I am a slam
Sweet enough to eat
A tasty treat
with blackberry jam
In between
Mean enough to be your
Overseer
See you through to victory
And unbirthed dreams
I am a slam
plush and soft
A word rush
To soothe your pain
Let loose the blame
I am a story to be sung
Not written or wrung
From dry pages
And past ages
I am a slam now

Anyhow
Against opposition and my own contrition
Let me state my position
new, unused, refuse to be abused
And free
I bleed a word melody...
SLAM! JAM!!
SLAM! JAM!
I AM

A story waiting to be freed...

PRAISE SONG FOR SONIA
In a poem at thirty
Sista Sonia said
she was always traveling--
traveling--
walking nights
into days;
did not always know
where she was going.
But traveling took her places
helped her fill the spaces
betwixt
sun-baked Alabama days
& New York's
adolescent
Long Island nights.
Touched by Malcolm's
thick-lipped dreaming
revolutionary lines,
she, too, composed Black rhetoric
posing points & asking us
hard questions 'bout
"who's gonna take the words."
Filling poems,
praise and chants
with immediacy...
touching her pulse--
our pulse--the world's pulse,
She said, "we be. gonna be
even after being. Black
mass has always been."

From Amherst to Nicaragua,
to elegies for MOVE,
to dispelling myths 'bout Black blues
by China's great wall,
Sista Sonia
braided twist of old adage
into new knots of wisdom
and implored—
screamed, shouted, chanted, sang--asked us,
"how does one scream into thunder?"
As it was written in Shigeko,
Sista Sonia, has been obliged.
Obliged to speak of Gwen Brooks.
Obliged to speak for Mamma.
Obliged to speak to fathers
and brothers
and sisters with whom
we've all shared watery soup.
Sista Sonia has been obliged
to loosen our scalps,
navigate wounds, wrap us in rage
& recovery;
to negotiate hypnotic sea shores
that belch waves like knowledge
of birth and death
to wash us all—tall
no longer ugly (like the 2nd and 3rd grade sisters)
but "napped-free"
from notions of "hair short",

"legs and face ashy."
Sista Sonia says
"a pretty little black girl lookin'
just like me."
In "To Whom It May Concern"
she warned yawl, "watch out for the full
moon of Sonia
shinin' down on ya...
she'll grind you down
leave greasy spots
all over yo soul till you bone dry/man"
all creased and tattooed
touched by her hand--
Sista Sonia can!
Embracing the symbolism
of butterflies
colored with diversity
eating the leaves of collard greens
from peopled-gardens
like Black folks with wings,
Sista Sonia asked us
"where is your fire"
and with a great roar
she tells us, "you got to find it,
and pass it on."
Angered by a life of crusts
for girls, or boys
or nations
or races,

celebrating essence,
she told us all
"Black women are violets
tied in bunches. Braids of hurt."
No.
"Not even the rust of Southern boundaries"
as she said, "could stop us".
Can't stop her,
Sista Sonia
bleeding
& resurrecting life
from the blood;
grooming poets
from the mud;
leading--
like Baldwin,
like Walker,
like Brooks,
like Sterling Brown.
No hers is not a small voice!

* previously published in *They Never Told Me There'd Be Days Like This*
(Three Goat Press: Darby)

WE BE
Conjuring
Naming incantation with "Nommo" -
Word power
Power of the word
in the utterance
giving life
shaping it,
framing it,
sometimes blaming it
daring to drain it of its guise -
inconstancy, injustice or
simply,
the political economy
in government lies.
"Fire-words"
Force-value
Valued force
Forcing you to
Validate the
Naming--
Calling into being
Claiming the right
To scream,
Shout,
Spout
Her story and
His story--
History's incongruence,
Its in-continuity,
Its "irony"

Played out in a poem, now
For all to hear and see.
Performance poets be wordsmiths,
"gut-utters",
linguistic magicians,
activating
invigorating
manipulating temporal planes
pop culture
mass minds (masterminds) and whole worlds
into vestiges of
new ways of seeing;
new ways of being;
forms of believing anew.
With the breath of life in us
Oyo-embodied voice
creating image with
"fire words" and sounds.
Literate rhetoriticians take
allegory, metaphor and simile
turning them around,
empowered with Afrocentric constructions
new use value -
using the same old tools
WORD
The voice of one
On which to build
Imagining a world anew.
With spell-bounding poetics,

Reconstituting, re-imagining, and re-inventing
Performance Poets
Help us see cultural folk
heroes and "she-roes" who
pass through the ages,
jump from the pages,
take to the stages
on the tip of tongues thundering priests
and priestess of Shango.
With razor sharp precision
guided by Ogun,
Prolific, proficient,
prosodic Aficionados
rap, chant, scat, rhyme,
sssssssssing/song and sermonize in accomplished
verbosity.
Using time-tested techniques of theatricality -
call-and-response,
symbolism,
physicality,
rhythm,
use of the drum,
beat,
body
language,
ritual spectacle,
musicality -
you can't run

from the sweet and sour
"truisms"
speech-shaman prescribed
"do-isms"
WE
be puttin' in your ear!
Listen for our watchword,
Password, call words
Street preaching
Calling on a Muse
with a decidedly
New World/
First World
African World View;
in lyric, epic, ode,
blank verse/free verse,
Hip-hop
"rap",
sonnet,
ballad,
rhymed-meter or villanelle,
Performance Poets
spin elegy,
popularize force words, fresh lines and
image-heavy,
image-filled phrases.
Shades of Zora.
Gripping audiences
by instigating, insinuating, or

prompting introspection.
We stitch stanzas
that leap off of the page
verbal "dextarians"
accentuating stress
and meter
turning recitation,
to a revolutionizing revolutionary
new kind of *old memory.*
Bard, lyrist, troubadour,
versifier, sometimes "soothsayer"—
post-modern personifer—
shedding minstrel cloaks,
playing at performance,
in Performances anything but play!
Tragedian
Caught
Having to live in
And speak through
Tragicomedy, indeed.
We be "Griot"
Doctoring,
Diagnosing
Giving voice to the voiceless
Working to heal with words
The gapping wounds of those of us
Like the son of man
The best of us

The least of us
even unknown.
Using the strictest rite of ritual
oral prescription,
We
be
Performance Poets--
armed to the teeth!
Ashe!

Chapter 13
Reflections on Crisis in the Motherland

CHECK THE RHYME/TERI ELLEN CROSS

DROUGHT

(based on a New York Times photograph of a mother
during Sudan's 2005 drought)
in death she bears him on her back
the journey dries the wetness on her cheeks
his weight brings back her body's memories
his swollen lips aching for sustenance

the journey dries the wetness on her cheeks
she remembers now his breath, harsh, hot, hungry
his swollen lips aching for sustenance how she
beat her flattened breasts

not only his breath, harsh, hot, hungry but
a stubbed rock skips and stirs memories of his kick
a belated twinge beats in her flattened breasts
so stubborn refusing to bear fruit

a stubbed rock's skip stirs memories of his kick
with each step does she will him alive, does she
forsake the earth too stubborn to bear her fruit,
the fruit plucked
in death she now bears on her back

CHECK THE RHYME/DEBRA POWELL-WRIGHT

SOUTHWEST TOWNSHIP

(for Hector Peterson and Faheem Thomas-Childs)
In the dry, white season of Soweto
Soldiers & civilians shared bartered beer for bullets

Biko's black consciousness languished between
Sarafina lives and South African language liberation
songs

Didn't take long for the common hood to be silenced &
Unpacified babies to morph into misunderstood youth

Missed education became the norm

Why ask how did the righteous get wronged?
Why ask how did the righteous get wronged?
Why ask how did the righteous get wronged?

In the moist, red, june of seventy-six
Hector's thirteen year old history,
housed in one photographic memory
Reminded mourners of red, black & green grief

South-west segregation made a way for
Shanty-town demoralization

Young warriors cried freedom on already
tear-stained roads
Their multi-colored blood can't distinguish
friend from foe

Do you know what's happening in your Soweto?
Do you know what's happening in your Soweto?
Do you know what's happening in your Soweto?

In the dark, shady aftermath of apartheid
Busing isn't easy for elders trying to vote with the rights
they've won
Gold-rush ghettos thrive in the name of truth and
reconciliation

New spoken words can't be heard
Political leaders don't always keep their word
Another revolutionary child has lost her life
Armed forces are unable to fight poverty & strife

There's no place for poor people
to find peace
on earth when
Their nationalists are exiled from their place of birth

Do you care what happens in your ghetto?
Do you care what happens in your ghetto?
Do you care what happens
In the dry, white season of Soweto?

Chapter 14
Reflections on Home

CHECK THE RHYME/RACHELLE ARLIN CREDO

ON A MOONLIT NIGHT

Peering through the window, water apple leaves
sway with the breeze; dancers of the night
with green veined fingers cast quirky shadows
against the cream-colored concrete walls.

Beneath them, i turn to the porcelain cup
in my hands, whirling the tinted water of
fresh picked tea leaves invisible under steam
before lushing up to quench my thirst.

I look up and marvel
as succulent water apples
bounce back and forth
from their wellspring
like little children
playing tug-of-war.

It's an ingenuous spectacle
of swollen receptacles and
calyces on chlorophyll clothes
and cellulose accessories.

With the wind swatting their soft skins,
I wonder how they held on
and remained firm with every blow.
Wouldn't they want to be free
and relish liberty on the ground?

CHECK THE RHYME/RACHELLE ARLIN CREDO

I lay my back on a soft cushion
as the reality finally convinces me
- life -
in its bare simplicity.
I simply smile.

RESTORATION PIECE

The dresser sits
in the bedroom corner, six months,
like a cut refusing to heal.

Pitted layers of varnish and paint
suppress the bare wood.
"Keep it. I don't want it."

He wasn't just talking
about the dresser.
Her only uncluttered space.

Relic and representation,
kept for sake of promises
made and dismissed
on a whim.

Driving home,
she stops off for scraper
and solvent, brushes and paint
left for another day.

New knobs of brass,
goose-neck lamp, electric
screwdriver with instructions
on the back of the card.

Holiday weekend:
extra day's grace;
Extra-Strength Tylenol; two
more trips to Canadian Tire.

CHECK THE RHYME/BETTY DOBSON

In less than a week
the goose sports a nylon scarf
and the brass gets buffed
by Hanes Her Way.

IF HOME WERE A SONG

"Dahil sa iyo
nais kong mabuhay
dahil sa iyo
hanggang mamatay…"
(excerpted from "Dahil Sa Iyo"
[Because of You],
a popular Philipino love ballad)

If home were a song
I would sing it to you
A lullaby, warm and sweet
A cavern containing
Ocean sounds and sand heaps
You could rest your head upon the floor
And listen to its heart beat

If home were a song
our tsinellas on the hollow floor would
Flutter like the brush on a snare drum;
The clink and clatter of kuchilyas
and tinidores
Would be our rattles
And the drone of my father's snore would be
The bass tone.

Above the percussion of our household
I would sing you a family meal:
After the milkfish has been fried,
The oil splattered across the kitchen wall,
The rice cooker will bubble and boil;

Sili, toyo and suka
Will be emptied into
Tiny platitos
While mom, dad and sister
Gather round
A wobbly table
That has traveled cross the country four times.

Then you would hear the
Contented mashing of mandibles
Sporadic talk
And kundimans being crooned
In the living room.

"Dahil sa iyo
nais kong mabuhay
Dahil sa iyo
hanggang mamatay
kung tunay man ako
ang alipinin mo
ang lahat ng ito
dahil sa iyo…"

If home were a song
You would hear
The silence full of love
Between mouthfuls and record tracks
And I would sing it to you,
Until you have had
Your fill

DISHES

I was doin' the dishes
scrubbin the pots
singin the blues
and washin' off tops
tee shirt on
hair curled in sweat
and in comes him
3'2 still shower wet
"mama, u r so pretty."
that's what he saw
here i am doin' dishes
smellin like joy
and in comes my
stretchmarks
my
pride and
my joy

Chapter 15
State of Our Society

HEROES
At first there was nothing.
and God said, "Let there be light,"
and here we are, in the
dark.
The world began in nothingness
null void.
Hardly different today.
Dark night
Blood in the streets
All I do in response is write this
worthless poem.
We live in a time of typhoons.
emotional whirlwinds.

We tear at each other's throats like
wild dogs.
The world
- our suicidal world -
is on a transplant list
waiting patiently in line for a
soul.
We are the world
We are the champions
who crucified christ
who burned joan
who denounced luther
who imprisoned galileo
who called washington a rebel

who shot lincoln
who killed gandhi
who murdered king
we are the heroes
who have desecrated ourselves.
I mourn not the loss of our innocence
but that our goodness was stillborn.
I mourn that we are callow
that we serve the basest of human vices within
ourselves.
That we gorge ourselves on the sour wine of
cowardice in the guise of self-respect.
We are gluttons when it comes to the bitter potion of
human intolerance
if there is such a thing.
We are broken.
Broken beyond repair.
Perhaps if we obliterate ourselves
we can begin anew
from the ash we become.

MISEDUCATION OF A NEW GENERATION
Miseducation of a new generation
that consistently thinks making it
means....being on BET, MTV, or any
type of TV or media type of thing.
Not realizing that those videos
are not free.
And that the images are scripted
and acted out by models who are
hired.
And that the cars in the videos
are on loan
just like the rest of the bling bling.
But they just haven't heard.
Miseducation of a new generation
that consistently thinks you ain't made
it until you got that huge break
and that success just comes on really
quick.
But they don't know that success takes
time.

They think rappers don't write.
They don't know the work that comes
behind a concert or tour schedule.
They don't know that it takes a lot of
people behind an artist to market that
person, or album effectively.
They don't see the value in trying to slowly
build a career path.

The miseducation of a new generation
just doesn't stop at the lost young soldiers
of street life, but those lost in the cracks
in "No Child Left Behind"-izm that pushes children
quickly through the system.
Though you have minimal reading.
and Math skills lacking.
And some mommas, grandmas, and other parents who
don't reinforce reading and other skills.
Because ain't they supposed to learn everything in the
school?

The miseducation of a new generation
just doesn't stop.
It whirls out of control.
It gets confronted with hate
by single mothers who don't want to listen
to the old school moms who have the knowledge that
might set them free.
Oh, I long for the days when momma's dragged
their children over to the libraries.
Where there was real homework, not just fill in sheets.

Where every one on the block had the right to help
educate your child.
Where encyclopedias were the norm
and where book reports gave you your imagination.
Not, now - when children are entertained by
television, radio, videos and movies.

Not, now - where children are graduating but
still lack basic life skills to get them through.
Not, now - where children who don't have the
proper resources like books, and programs designed to
inspire them, will be lost in the cracks.

What we gonna do?
Cause it's all our responsibilities, to be that
village, that helps raise the children to a whole
new level of artistry, intellectual skills, and
raise them so they can shine for all to see.
What we gonna do?
Blind shut our eyes.
Or just silently cry in amen corners?

AMERICA
Where is my country
I couldn't find it
Among the
Sea of debris and
Putrid toxic waters of
A place once called
Home

Where is my country
They need to know
That U.S. Citizen
Is now a synonym
For refugee

Where is my country
Who thinks
It's arrogant
Leadership wisdom
Is the golden ambrosia
Ejaculated from the loins
Of mythical Gods

The same line of thought
That nominates
Supreme court justices
Without judicial experience

Because it is highly possible

CHECK THE RHYME / MIKAYLAH SIMONE

We didn't elect
A sensitive man
Or a kind man
But don't tell me
We elected the
Same man
Whose ranch vacations
Are more important
Than the preservation
Of human life

I do hope Condoleezza
Found the right pair of shoes
On her shopping trip
As families cried for missing loved ones

FEMA's concern is appreciated
But they are
20 feet and 5 days too late
For thriving cities
Now washed away with crushed
Bloated bodies
And future aspirations

WHERE IS MY COUNTRY
If you find it
You let me know

Chapter 16
The Waters We've Crossed

THE SUN SHALL RISE AGAIN
Gulf Coast, my love
Please forgive my tardiness, better late, than not at all
Because you are amongst the fortunate
I didn't heed the Rwanda call
I left them to suffer; I will not do this to you
This is one time I will actually follow through
Together we will reconstruct, once again you will reign
I'm choosing in this wake to not let your dead be in vain
Bodies lay in the street, and were quoted as "road kill"
This of course brought a smile to those on capital hill
As the Republican said, "abort all black babies and cut crime"
Exactly what they did in Trans-Atlantic times
I take full responsibility and vow to restore tranquility
You shall triumph in your hour of weakness
It's your gift, your victorious uniqueness
I'm here to somehow be your flicker in the shadows of darkness
And with much success, you will finally see progress
I will immerse you in energy from those far and wide
Let their love be your guide
As they stand by your side and with you invoke pride

You were never invisible to me, you're my greatest discovery
Beautiful music shall form in you a new song
As proof you're strong, and in America you belong
You are a new canvas of creation
From your soil came the birth of African civilization
A great nation with a true heart of celebration
That in heaven shall receive full compensation

On those streets paved with gold your innovative souls
Will at last be revealed
And the hate and pain you've endured
Will eternally be concealed
Now in another time and place, and possession of a pale
face

You would not have endured
This horrendous disgrace
Together we shall embrace
God's unfaltering grace
I beg of your forgiveness
And now, let me be your aid
I know you are afraid and you feel betrayed
I was sent as God's gift to you
I'm here to help you cope
I'll be with you forever
        Love always, HOPE

NIGHTMARE
This is a nightmare
the nightmare that never stops
and there are NO heroes
only victims,
victims,
victims
Welcome to the terrordome
waking up to the first day
of the rest of your life
when you lose your home
your job
your babies
and everything
that made you feel
secure
secure
secure
Mother Nature's waters
washed it all away
and them jokers sittin' up there in
that White House
didn't do half of what they should
and what about the prayers of the
Christians who pray on Sunday?
and the Muslims who pray five times
a day?
and the Jews who pray on Saturday?
Did anyone feel their prayers?
And what about the babies who cannot
pray for themselves?

That's why the saying goes, "God watches over
babies and fools"
so you know some of them politicians
is covered too!
Where was the supernatural hand to lift the powerless?
where was magic and miracle to stop the mayhem?
Did the Almighty not hear the prayers,
the tears, the wails and the pounding of fists?
Why New Orleans? – everyone asked
Was it the stench of liquor or the lure of sex?
Was it the all night jazz or the spirit of voodoo?
Was it the natives or the tourists?
Was it the class division or the division of race?
Who called it down?
Who made it happen?
Hur-ri-cane
Hur-ri-cane
Hur-ri-cane

Watch how you treat your
neighbor
watch what you call yourself
If you are real greedy
you just might lose your wealth
race is just a marking
it don't tell your worth
if you laugh real haarrrd
you might heal your hurt

And what did we learn from all
of this?
That we – Americans are not invincible?

That no one cares about the poor, the elderly,
the sick
That the world is coming to an end
or this is the beginning of the next civil
rights era?
And if we learned that -
do you know which of our
civil rights were violated?

I remember like it was yesterday
the raising of the water
the climbing on top of roofs
the tree branches and bodies floating
in the river that used to be my street
I remember the voices of the military men –
cold and mean
saying , 'Get back, don't come any further or
we're going to have to shoot!'
when we wanted to leave that Dome
that terror dome
that dome filled with fear
and stench
and crying
and death
and hopelessness
and disease
and lack
and those suckas
called them – us – we
my people,
looters

and robbers,
called them, us, we my
people
refugees
and thugs
and gang bangers,
and the forsaken
and the lost
made us sound worthless
made us look like we
hadn't been torn up
from the inside out
made us feel so
not American

Chapter 17
To New Orleans, With Love

LAVEAU'S SOJOURN
hear me loosen from the alabaster
when crosses   all   lose   grounding

these feathers from the hoodoo's cock
craft delicate flakes not of snow

no more bus tours
no more trampling over my charms
above ground under water I am calcium
the jetty spirals in ruby mud & splinter

I can rest now

w/ plastic & cinderblock   the markings are bloated
inscribed w/ a telling mood

tusks & asses are the conjures kindling your grief

what could my spells do now?
the rattle is drifting between a roof & a river
my handsome messengers float
head down in ghetto fab white

all this   good for my sleep

I've not slept for a very long time

how   un/peaceful these gates were

the levees long lost purpose

      my neighbors   some
      were w/out a stone   anyway

you've given enough coins
      no more flowers now
      leave no single note for your heart doting & twinge

      jot not another cross   *please*

my pores are filled
too cemented w/ wants & reprisal

      when the water   subsides
      prayers will have bosomed
thus the freshness of cholera & myth   goes further

MISSING
when a relative
or friend dies
suddenly, and you think
back to the last
time you saw them
alive,
some sunny afternoon.
how casual you were,
exchanging pleasantries,
inanities, taking
your leave without
regrets, the promise
to keep in touch
quickly broken and
forgotten, till you
receive that shattering
phone call, and realize
you missed
your final chance
to say
eleven years
ago, in the French
Quarter, I had lunch
before my plane.
I always meant
to come back,

CHECK THE RHYME/BOBBI DYKEMA KATSANIS

spend more time among
her frizzy-braided daughters,
under dust-clotted ceiling fans
stirring her sticky air,
near trumpets wailing
in her house of blues,
with her unburied,
marble-vaulted dead.
now she's drowned,
that grand old lady
prostitute, New Orleans,
I won't see her
like
again.

ODE TO NEW ORLEANS
Corny, funny and splendid
I have found the right way to spot a train in the mist
Seethe with the moon underneath the flurry of a
Casablanca fan
Let the world embrace the essence of a languid outsider
So willing to be told
Yesterday's lies
Hold a balcony in your iris
An azalea in the crook of your knee
Remember how the sound of sizzling laughter
Helped you find new agbalagba, ancestors
Elders made of Texan horn and corn
New York's 19th Century's most beautiful Rose
Elders that hold you between them
Heal you with words and books
In frames of worn, browning images
With pecans, goat cheese, and ginger
Heal you with how their hopes
led them everywhere
and nowhere they expected
to be

Chapter 18
Violence Will Never Silence Us

CHECK THE RHYME/TERI ELLEN CROSS

UNDERSTOOD

Black women are not supposed to turn
Black men in for rape.
Never seen the rule but I know it's written down
somewhere maybe, underneath the threadbare sheets of
my twin bed, or on the stucco wall he threw me against.
Maybe it's behind the three weeks afterward
when I never left my apartment.
Maybe he just shook it out me and it crawled into some
gutter and hid out with all my no's, stop and please.
Can't recall where I've seen it or how I heard about it
but I know it's there like a scar I carry inside somewhere
I can't see, somewhere that still makes me cry
sometimes, especially when I hear he still breathes,
walks, and even wonders on occasion how I am

BANNED
You are not welcome here.
Our town fenced
the moment you step up to the border.

You will never be welcome here.
Rage a long time coming
entranced by its feverish burning
against the purple vistas
of my haven.

You are not welcome here
because you lied.
Said you didn't do
what I remember, the trial
convicted you of.

Don't hit your sister, girlfriend said.
I never did, you said
eyes wide in astonishment
remembering the high school football player
pummeling me into silence.

Your fists,
and feelings stillborn.
Some at the very top of the ceiling.
The other brother, the rapist,
at least left me some detritus on the ceiling.
Your fists, and I enter
non-existence.

You will never be welcome here.
This town never your sanctuary
this is my place, and the townspeople's place,
and batterers are not allowed.

Grisel Acosta is a multi-cultural writer originally from Chicago. She has a B.A. in journalism and a Master's Degree in English Education. Her writing, which ranges from poetry and plays to songs, news and feature articles, has been published and presented throughout the United States. Grisel's most recent projects have include: writing and producing "The Room," her play about class and race issues among women; directing "The Teacher's Lounge" for the Songs From Coconut Hill Playwrights Festival; and creating a panel discussion on the black Latino experience (this is part of her forthcoming creative non-fiction book on the same topic).

Naa Norley Adom was born to Ghanaian parents and raised in Spring Valley, New York. She is a recent graduate of Goucher College and currently enrolled in Hollins University's MFA program in Creative Writing. She writes because the pen doesn't have a tongue to trip over an "I love you," whether it's a private letter to her lover or an open letter to her people.

Lisa Ann Bailey has been writing and performing poetry for over ten years. She writes about social issues in the black community and the criminal justice system to help build cultural awareness and self esteem. For the past four years she has studied the art of writing in a Writer's Workshop given by noted poet Luis Reyes Rivera. She earned a Bachelor's Degree from John Jay College of Criminal Justice.

Crystal D. Baker was born in Dennison, TX. Crystal's poems have been featured in the anthology *Love and Luminaries*, *The International Library of Poetry*, *Sounds of Poetry* CD, *Best Poets of 2002*, *Theatre of the Mind* (Noble House) and the forthcoming book, *On the Wings of Poetry*. Crystal resides in Denver, CO with her husband Christopher Hill and lives happily with their two daughters Alexis, and My'auna. Using her maiden name as her pen name, she continues to write poetry and is presently working on her biggest writing challenge yet, a fiction novel entitled *Deadly Betrayal*.

Tiffany Woods Bennett was born January 15, 1974. She developed a passion for poetry around the age of 13. Over the years, her writing has developed from a therapeutic hobby, to a possible career alternative. She is a full time student seeking a Master's in Sociology. She has performed locally for several years including being featured on Public Access television and local radio stations. She resides in St. Louis, with her husband Robert Bennett.

Veronica Precious Bohanan (Moon) is a graduate of the University of Iowa, where she earned a B.A. in Speech and Hearing Sciences and an M.A. in Social Foundations of Education. She is a member of the Nommo Gathering Black Writers Collective, and half of the writing, performance, and artistic team of AquaMoon, a duo dedicated to providing a voice for disenfranchised women and youth. The team's choreopoem *Aqua Beats and Moon Verses* expresses this mission with its motto, 'Dismantling the Culture of Silence.' Continuing in this spirit, *Om: My Sistagyrl Lotus* is Ms. Bohanan's debut collection of poetry/prose.

Sharon Bridgforth is the Anchor Artist for The Austin Project (sponsored by The Center For African and African American Studies, U.T. Austin). Bridgforth, the Lambda Award winning author of *the bull-jean stories* and *love conjure/blues* (RedBone Press) has received support from: The National Endowment For The Arts/Theatre Communications Group Playwright in Residence Program; and the Rockefeller Foundation Multi-Arts Production Fun Award. For more information go to: www.sharonbridgforth.com.

Rachelle Arlin Credo is a fiction writer and poetry aficionado from the Philippines. Her poetry has recently been published in *Southern Ocean Review, Static Movement, Westward Quarterly, Lily Literary Review, Poetic Hours and The Renascent Vol. 2.*

Teri Ellen Cross graduated with a MFA in Creative Writing, Poetry from American University and a BS in journalism from

Ohio University. She is a graduate of Cave Canem - a weeklong poetry workshop for African American poets. She currently holds the position of poetry coordinator for the Folger Shakespeare Library in Washington D.C. She has had poems published in *Bum Rush The Page, Cave Canem: Gathering Ground, Growing Up Girl: An Anthology of Voices from Marginalized Spaces*, online at *Beltway Quarterly*, and in several Cave Canem anthologies.

In 2004, **Aya de Leon** was nearly elected in her one-woman show, "Aya de Leon is Running for President," and she was the *SF Chronicle's* best discovery in theater for her solo show "Thieves in the Temple: The Reclaiming of Hip Hop." That same year, the *SF Bay Guardian* gave her a Goldie award in spoken word. In 2005, she was voted "Slamminest Poet" in the *East Bay Express*. Aya has been an artist in residence at Stanford, a Cave Canem poetry fellow, she has appeared on HBO's Def Poetry Jam, and her work has been featured in *Essence*. Aya has released two spoken word CDs, and is currently working on a novel. Visit www.ayadeleon.com.

Writer, vocalist and sound artist, **LaTasha N. Nevada Diggs**, is the author of three chapbooks which include *Ichi-Ban and Ni-Ban* (MOH Press), and *Manuel is Destroying My Bathroom* (Belldonna Press) and has produced an audio project entitled, *Television*. LaTasha has received scholarships, residencies, and fellowships from Cave Canem, Harvestworks Digital Media Arts Center, Naropa Institute, Caldera Arts, and the New York Foundation for the Arts. La Tasha is the poetry curator for the online arts journal, www.exittheapple.com. teaches at Medgar Evers College.

Betty Dobson is an award-winning, published poet and the owner of InkSpotter Publishing. As a longtime volunteer, she donates her time and her talents to causes close to her heart, including adult literacy, AIDS awareness, and the prevention of violence against women. She shares her living space with an overgrown kitty who believes (rightly or wrongly) that he's the one in charge.

Patty Dukes is a phenomenal Hip-Hop Artist, Actress, Writer, Performer and Filmmaker from the South Bronx. As a freelance writer her words have graced the pages of *Urban Latino, The Ave, Kicksclusive* and *Fuego Magazine*. Patty is the recipient of both the 2005 Community Action Lab Grant from the Bronx Museum of the Arts to create The Girls Hip-Hop Project and Chica Luna Productions' 2005 F-Word Lab. Patty wrote and directed the short hip-hop film "On *Everything I Love.*" Patty works as a teaching artist for Dreamyard and Pepatian's Hip-Hop Academy. Her poetry and rhymes appear in the forthcoming book, *The Sistahood: On The Mic (*July 2006, Atria/Simon and Schuster) by debut novelist E-Fierce. Visit www.pattydukes.com

Writer and visual artist, **Cheryl Durgans** was raised in the tiny college town of Yellow Springs, Ohio. She received a B.A. degree in Art with a concentration in painting from Spelman College in Atlanta, GA. Now based in Philadelphia, PA, Cheryl is a candidate for a Master's Degree in Liberal Arts from the University of Pennsylvania. She has just completed her final thesis project, a speculative fiction novel and analysis based on the concept of Afrofuturism. She has participated in the Philadelphia Fringe Festival as both a writer and artist, and as a performer in the Philadelphia Black Women's Art Festival.

Originally from Toronto, **Zetta Elliot, PhD.** has spent the past ten years writing, teaching, and studying in the United States. She earned the Ph.D. in American Studies in 2003 at New York University. Her poetry and essays have been published in *Coloring Book: an Eclectic Anthology of Fiction and Poetry by Multicultural Writers* (Rattlecat Press), *T Dot Griots: an Anthology of Toronto's Black Storytellers* (Trafford Publishing), and *The Black Arts Quarterly.* She is currently a Visiting Professor of African American Literature in the English Department at Louisiana State University.

Natasha Ria El-Scari is a recently divorced mother of two children ages seven and two. She is the Project Director of Upward Bound at the University of Missouri-Kansas City. Recently, Natasha's sister and best friend died unexpectedly from a heart attack, and this changed her life greatly. In March, Natasha independently released her first poetry CD entitled, "DragonButterFirefly" shortly after her 30th birthday. This trailblazer has a passion for young people, art, and family and performs her work often.

Letitia Davis Ford was born in Guam in 1970 and traveled extensively at a young age. Reared in Montgomery, Alabama, Letitia attended Alabama State University. She began writing poetry in 1996 and after a few years of honing her craft, moved into fiction. Currently residing in North Atlanta, Letitia is hard at work on her first novel and first volume of poetry.

A Louisiana native, born and raised in Baton Rouge, **Amani Francis** currently resides in Jacksonville, Florida with her husband and daughter where she is a Professor of English at Florida Community College at Jacksonville. She is the author of *Nannie Eva*, a member of Culture Moves 101 West African Dance Company and co-editor of *Venue* – A Southern Literary e-Journal. At the present time, Amani is writing a novel with her colleague Terri Staten, and is also planning a sequel to *Nannie Eva*.

DuEwa Frazier is a poet, author, speaker and educator. She is the author of: *Goddess Under the Bridge, Ten Marbles and a Bag to Put Them In: Poems for Children,* Shed*ding Light From My Journeys* and *Stardust Tracks on a Road.* DuEwa earned the M.Ed. Degree in Curriculum and Teaching from Fordham University and the M.F.A. in Creative Writing degree from The New School. Her work has featured in *Tidal Basin Review, Reverie Journal, Kweli Journal, Poetry In Performance, Essence Magazine, X Magazine* and others. Visit her websites at www.duewaworld.com and Twitter.com/duewa1.

Shamarra Garmon is a 25-year-old writer whose poetry is a testimony of her past, present and future. She resides in Woodson, Arkansas.

Silvia Gonzalez S. is an award-winning playwright whose plays have been performed in New York, Los Angeles, Chicago, Texas, Arizona, Oregon and more. Her well-produced plays include: *El Vagon, Boxcar, Alicia in Wonder Tierra (Or I Can't Eat Goat Head)*, and *The Migrant Farmworker's Son*. Silvia's other achievements include: Kennedy Center New Visions New Voices Award, Oregon Arts Commission Fellowship Award, a Sundance Film option, a Lila Wallace/Readers Digest Grant Award and an Honorable Mention in the HBO's Writer Project.

Hadiyah Nicole Green, a St. Louis, Missouri native, is the author of a collection of poetry, observations, and self-realizations entitled *I FLOW*. Her poetry has been recognized by the International Library of Poetry: Poet of the Year for 2005 nominee and Honorary Member of the International Society of Poets for 2005. Hadiyah Nicole obtained a B.S. Degree in Physics from Alabama Agricultural & Mechanical University. She has received honors including: National Science Foundation Bridge to Doctorate Graduate Fellowship recipient and NASA Space Grant Consortium Scholarship recipient. She is a candidate for the Ph.D. in Physics at The University of Alabama at Birmingham.

Deborah D. Grison (Collage) is a Spring 2006 Candidate for the MFA in Creative Writing/Poetry at Sarah Lawrence College. She has been writing for 19 years and has published one volume of poetry, *THE ATTIC: words from the top* (2001). It received an endorsement from renowned poet, Nikki Giovanni and Reggie Gibson from the movie, "Love Jones." Collage has shared stages with poetry legends such as the Last Poets, Sonia Sanchez, and Gwendolyn Brooks and performed at various colleges and universities across the country. She currently lives and loves in NJ.

Nivedita Gunturi is originally from Dallas, Texas. She is a senior majoring in English at Tufts University, in Medford, Massachusetts and will be attending medical school in India in the fall. Nivedita enjoys reading classic literature and singing Indian classical music. She hopes to be able to use her writing and her role as a physician to instigate social change.

Ellen Hagan is a writer, actress and educator. Her poetry has been nominated for a Pushcart Prize and can be seen in *Failbetter, La Petite Zine, nervygirl* and *Monologues for Women by Women*. Her performance work has been produced by Spokenworks for the ROAR Theatre Festival, New York International Fringe Festival and the American Living Room Festival. She recently performed for Season 5 of *Russell Simmons Presents Def Poetry Jam* and is currently touring with a two-woman show, *Becoming Woman*. Ellen holds an MFA in fiction from The New School University, and is working on a full-length novel entitled *The Kentucky Notes/Notes Home*.

Bobbi Dykema Katsanis is currently a doctoral student in Art and Religion at the Graduate Theological Union in Berkeley, California. Her work has been published in *Rock & Sling, Ruah, Sacred Journey*, and *Alive Now*. Her first chapbook, *The Magdalene's Notebook*, is forthcoming this year from Finishing Line Press.

Maria D. Laso is a Cuban American writer of creative fiction and dreamer of dreams. She is founder of chixLIT, a bimonthly literary 'zine created by and for chix ages 7 to 17. chixLIT's motto is, "Words are powerful, and they can make you powerful too." Visit her website at www.chixLIT.com.

Tamara Madison is a writer, poet, and performer living and working in Georgia. She is the author and performer of *Naked Voice*, the 2002 winner of the First Literary Recording Contest sponsored by AUTHENTIC VOICEwork Records. Tamara has recorded as a bilingual poet and songstress on the self-titled CD, "JUBA Collective" (Premonition Records), an internationally performing and multidisciplinary, touring arts ensemble from Chicago. She has worked as a teaching artist, leading workshops and residencies for agencies including Fulton County Arts Council. She is currently completing a manuscript and a one-woman stage piece as companion to her solo CD project.

Keisha J. Moore (Lady Laureate) is a poet, an activist, a performance artist and an actress, who resides in Columbia, SC. She has been exploring the art of poetry for over 15 years. She strives to challenge conventionalism with creativity. Her work has been published in several literary journals and anthologies, and she has performed at the Furious Flower Poetry Center at James Madison University. Keisha is currently completing a CD, and a collection of poetry.

An emerging poet from Jackson, Tennessee, **Kimberly S. Morris** is a clinical social worker at Middle Tennessee State University. She is also a member of the Griot Collective Poetry Workshop of West Tennessee.

Thailan Nguyen is a Vietnamese and Chinese poet, born in a refugee camp outside of Bangkok. Her name means "peaceful flower." She came to American at the age of two. She sings in two bands: a Berlin-based live Hip Hop ensemble called Long Lost Relative and a local Brooklyn project called, A Billion Stars (psychedelic/spoken word ala Jim Morrison meets Godspeed). She resides in Brooklyn, New York.

Solimar Otero, Ph.D. is a Cuban /Puerto Rican American ethnologist by training. She received her Ph.D. in Folklore and Folklife from the University of Pennsylvania. Otero is a scholar of African Diaspora Studies with a specialization in Religious Folklore and Latino Caribbean Literature. She has conducted ethnographic research in Havana, Cuba and in Lagos, Nigeria as a Fulbright Researcher. Her work has been published in *Africa Today* and *The Black Scholar*. Otero is currently working on a book, *Orunile: Heaven is Home, Afrolatino Diasporas in Africa and the Caribbean.*

Pat McLean-RaShine teaches adult & teen workshops at Temple University's Pan-African Studies Community Education Program and Drexel University. She is an award-winning poet presently performing with In The Company Of Poets, a group which she founded. Pat has appeared on TV and radio, and is the author of two self-published books of poetry; *A Sister Speaks Of...* and *Ain't Gonna Bite My Tongue No More*. Pat has a collection of short stories entitled *Healing Her Hurts*. Visit her website at www.patmclean.com.

Originally from Canada, poet, songwriter, actress, **Karen Gibson Roc** and her band Fluid have performed with the likes of Patti Labelle, Sheila E. and The Commodores for *Glamorama* a spectacular fundraiser at the Chicago Theatre in Minneapolis. Karen has also graced such stages as HBO'S Def Poetry Jam, The Brooklyn Academy of Music, Central Park Summerstage w/Lyricist Lounge, S.O.B.'S, Joes' Pub, C.B.G.B.'s, and many more. She is featured on "Future Waves of Black Folks" by Champion Soul/remixed by Giles Peterson, released by Main Squeeze. Visit www.karengibsonroc.com.

Alicia Benjamin-Samuels was born in Washington, D.C. and raised in the Wilmington, Delaware area. Her poems have appeared in London's *X Magazine*, *Black Arts Quarterly*, *WarpLand*, Philadelphia's *Open City: A Journal of Community Arts and Culture*, Yale University's *Black Ivy*, and

Web-zines: The Eintouist, SeeingBlack.com, and The New Verse News. She resides in Nashville, Tenn. with her husband and daughter.

Queen Sheba (Bethsheba A. Rem) is a Spoken Word master poetess based in Norfolk, VA, who is the founder and CEO of Oya Xclusive a spoken word recording company in Norfolk, VA. Queen Sheba has successfully released three spoken word CDs, "I Confess", "The Message", and "The Truth". In 2002, Queen Sheba graced the stages of BET's 106th & Park and Apollo's Amateur Night. Queen Sheba has a worldwide following of poetry enthusiasts; presently hosting a very successful weekly venue and annual concerts that boast an estimated 1,000 audience members every show.

As a New Yorker and Texas native, **Mikaylah Simone** displays her liberating experimental form in her debut book of poetry "My Manufactured English." Her provocative poetic style embraces cultural identity as she intermingles Swahili roots with modern issues of politics, religion, violence, community and the complexity of love; all revealing the fresh insight of this author's journey that is honest, sad, comical and true. Visit www.msimone.com.

Mocha Sistah is an accomplished writer with nine publishing credits including her latest chapbook, *Tears of Woman: The Light Within.* Her work has featured in *Black Romance Magazine* and *My Soul To His Spirit Anthology* (SoulDictates Publishing). Winner of the 2004 Gwendolyn Brooks Poetry Award, she works in the area of literary arts education as an Artist-In-Residence with the Poetry Center of Chicago, Chicago Children's Museum and other institutions. Visit www.mochasistahonline.com.

Aimee Suzara is a Filipina-American poet/performer, cultural worker, and arts educator. An M.F.A. candidate at Mills College, and a youth and woman's advocate, Suzara has been featured as a spoken word artist at venues throughout the San Francisco Bay Area and beyond. Recently, her work was included in a CD release, "Eye of the Storm," to benefit families affected by Hurricane Katrina, and she was invited to perform part of her one-woman-show-in-progress, which explores the concept of returning "home," at CounterPULSE's STREAMfest in April 2006.

Leah Suzensky is a 23 year-old poet whose writing is fueled by the necessity for young black women to have a voice. Her influences include Maya Angelou, Nikki Giovanni, Sonia Sanchez and Langston Hughes. She plans to attend school for Africana Studies. She resides in Pittsburgh, PA.

Stacey Tolbert is affectionately known as the "Brown Suga Poet." Tolbert is the author of *Baring My Soul* and the 2004 recipient of the San Diego Journalism Press Club Award. Tolbert is the playwright of *A Quarter Past The Blues*, and spoken word artist on her "The Awakening" CD. She is a freelance writer, motivational speaker and workshop facilitator of Healertainment and Sistainment Girls' Group workshops. She resides in Kansas.

Ella Turenne is an artist, activist and educator. She is a board member of the Blackout Arts Collective and a co-founder of SistaPac Productions. Ella was recently featured in *Letters From Young Activists: Today's Rebels Speak Out* and is working on the completion of her first poetry manuscript and screenplay. She was last seen in the experimental film, "Big, Dark, Scary Girl." For more information, please visit www.blackwomyn.com.

Lorene Delany-Ullman is a native Californian, and earned her M.F.A. from the Graduate Program in Writing at University of California, Irvine. She has been published in *Elixir, Crab Creek Review, Washington Square*, Identitytheory.com and *Perihelion*. She currently teaches composition and poetry at the University of California, Irvine.

She is also one of the founding members of the Casa Romantica Poetry Reading Series in south Orange County.

Jamila Zahra Wade is a teacher, writer, and artist whose poetry appears in *I Woke Up and Put My Crown On* and *Bum Rush the Page: A Def Poetry Jam*. A native of the Roxbury neighborhood of Boston, MA, Jamila graduated from Spelman College and holds a Master's of Education Degree from Harvard University. She is the Executive Director of a creative writing organization that serves children and youth in Southeast, Washington, DC.

Jamie Walker, Ph.D. is a poet, noted journalist, scholar, and author of the favorably reviewed book, *101 Ways BlackWomen Can Learn to Love Themselves*. Walker is also the author of *Signifyin' Me: New and Selected Poems* (2006) and editor of *Sonia On My Mind: A Collection of Scholarly Essays and Literary Criticism*. Her work has featured in publications, including *BMa: The Sonia Sanchez Literary Review*. She teaches African American Literature at Bowie State University and Howard University, where she recently earned the Ph.D.Degree in African American Literature. She has received fellowships from The Lannan Poetry Foundation and The National Visionary Leadership Project. She resides in Washington, D.C.

Donna Weaver is a graduate of The University of Pittsburgh with a B.A. in English Writing. She was awarded the Scott Turow Prize for fiction in 2003. Donna was accepted to the Catskills Writing Workshop in 2002 with a scholarship and the 2005 *Cave Canem African American Poet's Summer Writing Retreat*. Her work has recently appeared in or is forthcoming from *Kota Press, Loop, Whimperbang, Poetry Motel,* and others. Donna is currently finishing her creative nonfiction manuscript *A Lot of Girl Falling*. She is editor-in-chief of *Caketrain Journal and Press*.

CHECK THE RHYME/BIOGRAPHIES

Niama Leslie Williams, Ph.D. recently earned her doctorate in African American Studies from Temple University; she also possesses degrees in comparative literature and professional writing. Her work has appeared in *Dark Eros, Spirit & Flame, Catch the Fire, Beyond the Frontier, Tattoo Highway #6, P.A.W. Prints*, and most recently in *Mischief, Caprice, and Other Poetic Strategies* (Red Hen Press). Visit her website at www.niamalesliewilliams.citymax.com.

Treasure Williams is a Memphis based writer, freelance editor, journalist, M.C., and emerging poet. She is the Memphis editor of the *Drumvoices Revue* and a Cave Canem fellow. Her performance abilities have been showcased on National Public Radio's *All Things Considered,* and Turner South's *"My South Speaks"* television commercial. She has an MFA from The University of Memphis. The included poems are from her manuscript, *resurrecting remains.*

Kimmika L.H. Williams-Witherspoon, Ph.D. (Anthropology); MA (Anthropology); MFA (Theater); Graduate Certificate (Women's Studies); B.A. (Journalism) is currently Head of Undergraduate Advising and an Assistant Professor of Theater History in the Theater Department at Temple University. Williams-Witherspoon is the 2000 winner of the $50,000 PEW Charitable Trusts Fellowship in the Arts for Scriptwriting, among other awards. Williams-Witherspoon is the author of seven books of poetry including: *They Never Told Me There'd Be Days Like This (2002);* and *Signs of the Time: Culture Pop, (1999).*

Debra Powell-Wright's love for writing and performing poetry comes from her recognition and appreciation of the power of sounds and words. Whether reciting a poem in the form of a sestina, with her In The Company of Poets partner, or doing a husband and wife acoustic set with Nagohead's world beat poetry and songs, Debra take her creative endeavors seriously and joyfully. She resides in Philadelphia.

NOTES

♦ **Lit Noire Publishing Books** ♦

<u>Order online via</u>

www.Lulu.com

www.Amazon.com

Thank you for your support!

CPSIA information can be obtained
at www.ICGtesting.com
Printed in the USA
LVHW101913130722
723344LV00001B/45